# THE LIFE OF
# SAINT JOSEPH
## AS SEEN BY THE MYSTICS

# COMPILED BY PAUL THIGPEN

# THE LIFE OF SAINT JOSEPH

## AS SEEN BY THE MYSTICS

*From the Visions of*
SAINT BRIDGET OF SWEDEN,
SERVANT OF GOD MARINA DE ESCOBAR,
VENERABLE MARY OF ÁGREDA,
VENERABLE MARIA CECILIA BAIJ
*and* BLESSED ANNE CATHERINE EMMERICH

Compiled by
*Paul Thigpen*

TAN Books
Gastonia, North Carolina

Excerpts from the English translation of the *Catechism of the Catholic Church*, Second Edition, © 1994, 1997, 2000 by Libreria Editrice Vaticana–United States Catholic Conference, Washington, D.C. All rights reserved.

Cover design by Andrew Schmalen

Cover image: St. Joseph, Guercino (Giovanni Francesco Barbieri) / Bridgeman Images

Library of Congress Control Number: 2022943625
ISBN: 978-1-5051-2290-9
Kindle ISBN: 978-1-5051-2291-6
ePUB ISBN: 978-1-5051-2292-3

Published in the United States by
TAN Books
PO Box 269
Gastonia, NC 28053
www.TANBooks.com

Printed in India

### For Michael Borja
*Devoted husband of my daughter, loving father of my grandchildren, and imitator of Saint Joseph*

"I give you these visions, not for yourself; they are given to you so that they may be recorded. I give you these visions—and I have ever done so—to prove that I shall be with My Church till the end of days. But visions alone sanctify no one; you must practice charity, patience, and all the other virtues."
—Jesus to Blessed Anne Catherine Emmerich

# CONTENTS

*Declaration of Obedience* . . . . . . . . . . . . . . . . . . . . *ix*

Introduction . . . . . . . . . . . . . . . . . . . . . . . 1

1. The Early Life of Joseph . . . . . . . . . . . . . . . . 15
2. The Wedding and the Early Days in Nazareth . . . . 22
3. The Annunciation and the Visitation . . . . . . . . 30
4. Joseph Learns of Mary's Child . . . . . . . . . . . . 36
5. The Journey to Bethlehem . . . . . . . . . . . . . . 43
6. The Nativity . . . . . . . . . . . . . . . . . . . . . . . 54
7. The Shepherds' Visit and the Circumcision of Jesus . 61
8. The Visit of the Magi . . . . . . . . . . . . . . . . . . 70
9. The Presentation in the Temple . . . . . . . . . . . 81
10. The Flight into Egypt . . . . . . . . . . . . . . . . . 86
11. Life in Egypt . . . . . . . . . . . . . . . . . . . . . . 96
12. The Return to Nazareth . . . . . . . . . . . . . . . 106
13. Jesus in the Temple . . . . . . . . . . . . . . . . . . 112
14. Joseph's Later Years . . . . . . . . . . . . . . . . . 117
15. The Death of Joseph . . . . . . . . . . . . . . . . . 125
16. The Special Virtues, Graces, and Glories of Joseph . 133

*Sources* . . . . . . . . . . . . . . . . . . . . . . . . . *137*

*Other Recommended Reading* . . . . . . . . . . . . . . . *139*

# DECLARATION OF OBEDIENCE

IN conformity with the decrees of Pope Urban VIII concerning the publication of private revelations, I herewith declare that:

1. While the sources from which this book has been compiled have frequently been published with the approval of learned theologians and with the permission of the ordinaries of many dioceses in several countries, I willingly submit all that is contained in this work to the judgment of the Holy See;

2. In applying the terms "saint" and "venerable" to persons who are neither canonized nor beatified, I wish in no way to anticipate the final decision of the Church; and

3. For all the private revelations and seemingly supernatural events herein narrated, insofar as they have not received the attestation of the Church, I claim no more than the assent of a merely human credence, according to the dictates of prudence and the principles of mystical theology.

THE COMPILER

# INTRODUCTION

SINCE ancient times, Christians have wondered about so many things that the Gospel writers passed over in silence. We hear from the Evangelists, for example, very little about the life of the Holy Family; that is particularly the case with Saint Joseph.

Mark does not speak of him at all. John mentions him only in quoting those who referred to Jesus as his son (Jn 1:45; 6:42). Matthew and Luke tell us a bit more about the husband of Mary. But this mysterious saint disappears from Matthew's narrative after he brings Mary and the Child Jesus back from Egypt (Mt 2:23), and he is absent from Luke's account after Jesus is found in the Temple at the age of twelve (Lk 2:51).

Even in Matthew and Luke, no words of Saint Joseph are recorded. Nothing is told of his early life; nothing of his later years. No mention is made of his death, which occurred, apparently, sometime before Jesus began His public ministry.

Not surprisingly, speculations attempting to fill in the gaps of the saint's story date back to the early years of the Church. The so-called *Gospel of James*, composed around the year 150 (about fifty years after the composition of John's Gospel), provides us with some of the earliest conjectures of this sort. It may in fact draw in part on certain historical traditions as well.[1]

After the early centuries, such apocryphal texts with elaboration on the life of Saint Joseph gave way to claims of private revelations from God that seemed to supply some of what was lacking in the Gospel accounts. Several women religious, beginning in the medieval period, have left us with records of such visions. *The Life of Saint Joseph as Seen by the Mystics* crafts a narrative of the saint's life by drawing from the private revelations reported by five of these visionaries: Saint Bridget of Sweden (c. 1303–73), Venerable Marina de Escobar (1554–1653), Venerable Mary of Ágreda (1602–65), Venerable Maria Cecilia Baij (1694–1766), and Blessed Anne Catherine Emmerich (1774–1824). This work can be viewed as a companion volume to *The Life of Mary as Seen by the Mystics*, compiled by Raphael Brown (TAN Books, 1991).

## The Value of the Visions

In meditating on the visions of these mystical writers, we must use great discretion, recognizing that their value is primarily spiritual. Though the authors were by no means doctors of history, science, or theology, they were in many ways doctors of the soul. They display at times a fine understanding of the inner workings of the human mind and heart, and the influences of grace.

In their visions, then, we see not only Joseph, Jesus, Mary, and their contemporaries but in a certain sense ourselves as well. Held up as a mirror, this story invites us all to view ourselves more clearly and to imitate their holy example as we seek to navigate the course of our lives. It allows us as well to recognize our eternal debt to Saint Joseph as the guardian of our Savior and spouse of His mother. And it reveals to us the ways in which his heroic life and grace-filled death have

---

[1]    Also known as the *Book of James* or the *Protoevangelium*. See "Book of James," in F. L. Cross and E. A. Livingstone, eds., *The Oxford Dictionary of the Christian Church*, 2nd ed. (*Oxford*: Oxford University Press, 1983), 723.

made him a great patron for each of us in each hour of our lives—and especially at the hour of our death.

At the same time, we should keep in mind that the Catholic Church speaks of divine revelation with regard to two kinds. *Public* (or *universal*) revelation is that revelation contained in the Sacred Scripture and Sacred Tradition transmitted by the Church. Together, Scripture and Tradition form the one sacred deposit of the word of God.

This deposit was complete with the close of the apostolic age. "No new public revelation," says the *Catechism*, "is to be expected before the glorious manifestation of our Lord Jesus Christ."[2] All Catholics are obliged to believe public revelation as it is authentically interpreted by the Sacred Magisterium.

Certain *private* (or *particular*) revelations, on the other hand, have come to individuals from God down through the ages of the Church. "They do not belong," notes the *Catechism*, "to the deposit of faith. It is not their role to improve or complete Christ's definitive Revelation, but to help live more fully by it in a certain period of history."[3]

Nevertheless, some private revelations have been recognized by the authority of the Church. When the Church approves such revelations, she declares that nothing in them is contrary to faith or good morals and that they may be read without danger, read even with profit. Even then, however, Church approval imposes no obligation on Catholics to believe these revelations. With regard to such messages, Pope Benedict XIV has observed: "It is not obligatory nor even possible to give them the assent of Catholic faith, but only of human faith, in conformity with the dictates of prudence, which presents them to us as probable and worthy of pious belief."[4]

Regrettably, some readers have treated the visions of these mystical writers as if they were somehow infallible, a kind of fifth Gospel. We must avoid that mistake. In fact, the texts

---

[2]    *Catechism of the Catholic Church*, 2nd ed. (Vatican City: Liberia Editrice Vaticana, 1997), no. 66; *Dei verbum*, 4; cf. 1 Timothy 6:14; Titus 2:13. Hereafter referred to as "*CCC*."

[3]    *CCC* 67.

[4]    Pope Benedict XIV, *De canon.*, III, liii, xxii, II.

themselves, taken together, will not allow such an interpretation: Some aspects of the various visions cannot be reconciled.

Mary of Ágreda reported, for example, that both of Mary's parents had died by the time she and Joseph were betrothed. Anne Catherine Emmerich, on the other hand, spoke of Saint Anne's remarriage after Joachim's death and described her extensive involvement in the life of the Holy Family. How, we might ask, could these alleged private revelations truly be from God if they obviously display such inconsistencies among themselves—not to mention certain historical inaccuracies?

The Jesuit scholar Fr. Auguste Poulain, in his classic treatise on mystical theology, explains:

> When visions represent historic scenes . . . they often have an approximate and probable likeness only. . . . It is a mistake to attribute an absolute accuracy to them. . . . Many saints have, in fact, believed that the event took place exactly as they saw it. But God does not deceive us when He modifies certain details. If He tied Himself down to absolute accuracy in these matters, we should soon be seeking to satisfy in visions an idle desire for erudition in history or archaeology. He has a nobler aim, that of the soul's sanctification. . . . He is like a painter who, in order to excite our piety, is content to paint scenes in his own manner, but without departing too far from the truth.

The scholar-priest adds an important note: "This argument cannot be applied to the historical books of the Bible."[5]

Father Poulain goes on to observe that "God has another reason for modifying certain details. Sometimes He adds them to a historical scene in order to bring out the secret meaning of the mystery. The actual [historical] spectators saw nothing similar. . . . We see, therefore, that it is imprudent to seek to remake history by the help of the saints' revelations."[6]

---

[5]    Auguste Poulain, *The Graces of Interior Prayer, a Treatise on Mystical Theology* (St. Louis: B. Herder, 1912), Part IV, "Revelations and Visions," 327–29.
[6]    Poulain, 327–29.

To summarize, then: God might use a kind of artistic license in the visions or locutions He prompts. At the same time, certain inconsistencies or even errors may be introduced by the visionaries themselves or by others. Father Poulain suggests several possibilities.

First, the human mind of the visionary may mix some of its own thoughts, images, and impressions with those received from God, including certain favorite or preconceived ideas. Second, the record of divine revelation may be altered when the visionaries write or dictate it at a later time, or those who act as secretary may introduce either errors or their own thoughts not found in the original. Third, a printed text may be an incomplete version or inaccurate translation of the original manuscript.[7]

Yet another consideration: Spiritual writings may have difficulties arising from terminology. As Saint Robert Bellarmine observed: "Writers on mystical theology are usually blamed by some and praised by others because what they say is not understood in the same way by all."[8]

For all these reasons, then, we should view these writings as a kind of spiritual drama prompted by God: The events described, though offered in reference to historical events, are presented through an angle of vision akin to that of the poet, the novelist, the playwright, or the film director, rather than the historian, the scientist, the philosopher, or the theologian. We find here a fusion of realistic detail and mystical imagery, such as we might encounter in the best of visionary cinema.

## Priorities for Creating This Compilation

To craft this narrative, I compared the original texts and various translations of the primary sources whenever possible. Based on these, I combined, condensed, and adapted into a single style and voice many narrative threads from each mystical account.

---

[7]    Poulain, 323–40.
[8]    Quoted in Edward A. Ryan, "Foreword," in Raphael Brown, comp., *The Life of Mary as Seen by the Mystics* (1951; repr., Charlotte, NC: TAN Books, 1991), xii.

In selecting from among the many threads available, and in weaving them together into a single story, I have kept several priorities in mind.

First, since all but one of the works consulted were primarily focused on Our Lord, the Blessed Virgin, or other subjects, I had to draw from those texts the particular passages that had special relevance to Saint Joseph. In these pages you will find visions of his interior and exterior life: his thoughts, words, and attitudes; his character, deeds, and impact on others.

In some scenes included here, though he is always an essential figure in the story, Joseph appears only in passing or in the background. But of course that is how the good saint most often appears in the Gospels as well. In his great humility, he is no doubt content with that modest position.

Second, when I had to choose between the various visionaries' accounts of a particular event or scene, I drew from the one that seemed to me the richest, or the most profound, or the most beautiful. This was necessarily a subjective decision on my part, but unavoidable. Where possible, I wove together, even within the same sentence or paragraph, elements from various accounts. (For this reason, it was not feasible to footnote the source of each thread; a complete list of the sources is provided.)

At times, as we have noted, the details of various accounts did not agree. In that case, I omitted them or included those that were most in keeping with the arc of the overall story as presented.

Most readers will probably know the general outline of the Gospel accounts with regard to the events in Our Lord's life in which Saint Joseph appears. Those events are obviously part of this narrative, but the focus here is on details of the visions that do not appear in Scripture. It may be useful to read again, before taking up this book, the first two chapters of Matthew's Gospel and the first three of Luke's.

Before moving on to the story of the man who served as Christ's adoptive father here on earth, we should acquaint ourselves with each of the visionaries involved in this account so we can place them in their historical and spiritual context.

## Saint Bridget of Sweden (c. 1303–73)

Bridget (Birgitta; not to be confused with Saint Brigid of Ireland) was born in Sweden about 1303 to the family of a provincial governor. She married at the age of fourteen, becoming in time the mother of eight children. In 1343, her devout husband, Ulf Gudmarsson, entered a Cistercian monastery and died the following year.

After some years at the court of the Swedish king, Bridget established a new religious community of both women and men, the Order of the Most Holy Savior, now known as the Bridgettines. She went to Rome in 1349, where she spent most of her days until her death in 1373. Her fervent devotion, her charitable works, and her stern admonitions to certain powerful men of her day spread the fame of her holiness, and Pope Boniface IX canonized her in 1391.

From an early age, Bridget experienced heavenly visions. She began dictating her revelations and prophecies to one of her spiritual directors, which primarily concerned the sufferings of Christ and events that were about to happen in various kingdoms. These "Heavenly Revelations" fill nine volumes with more than 1,500 pages, and they were among the most popular books in late medieval Europe.

Pope Benedict XIV (1675–1758) declared that "there is no doubt: the Revelations of Bridget are included among those which have the approval of the Church; they are orthodox." As with other private revelations, however, this formal approval means only that they contain nothing contrary to faith and morals and that there is good evidence for their authenticity.[9]

More recently, Pope Saint John Paul II (1920–2005) observed in the apostolic letter *Spes Aedificandi*, which declared Saint Bridget as one of the co-patronesses of Europe: "There is no doubt that the Church, which recognized Bridget's holiness without ever

---

[9]  Alban Butler, *Lives of the Saints*, ed. Herbert Thurston and Donald Attwater (New York: P. J. Kenedy and Sons, 1963), vol. IV, 56–58.

pronouncing on her individual revelations, has accepted the overall authenticity of her interior experience."[10]

## Venerable Marina de Escobar (1554–1653)

Venerable Marina de Escobar was born into a pious and well-connected family in Valladolid, Spain. Her father, noted for his learning and saintly life, was a professor of civil and canon law and for a time served as ruler of the town of Osuna. Her mother was the daughter of the physician of the Holy Roman Emperor Charles V.

Marina was given to study, and from her early years, she showed considerable intellectual gifts. In her youth, she often experienced seasons of spiritual fervor, dryness, and scruples. She offered herself completely to God at the age of thirty-three, during the Lent of 1587.

After becoming bedridden, Marina spent the last thirty years of her life in a small, dark, poorly ventilated room, though Mass was daily celebrated for her in an adjacent room. Through her conversations with the small group of pious women who cared for her, they came to see her as their spiritual mother. Before her death, she was instrumental in founding the Spanish Bridgettine religious order.

During these same years, Marina often conversed as well with God, the angels, and the saints. These conversations are recorded in the book *The Marvelous Life of the Venerable Virgin Doña Marina de Escobar*, which includes accounts of visits from Saint Joseph. By divine command, as she believed, Marina wrote down her revelations, and when she became too feeble to write, she dictated them. One of her spiritual directors, Fr. Luis de Ponte, arranged them for publication after her death.

Father de Ponte bestowed high praise on both Marina's life and her visions. He believed her personal holiness was an indication that the revelations were genuine. She was advanced in virtue, he noted; preserved free from temptations against

---

[10] Pope Benedict XVI, "Saint Bridget of Sweden, General Audience, October 27, 2010; https://www.vatican.va/content/benedict-xvi/en/audiences/2010/documents/hf_ben-xvi_aud_20101027.html.

purity; showed no pride; had peace in prayer; feared deception; desired no extraordinary divine favors; loved suffering; was zealous for souls; and was obedient to her confessor.[11]

## Venerable Mary of Ágreda (1602–65)

Mary Coronel entered the convent in Ágreda, Castile, Spain, as a teenager and took the name Mary of Jesus. By the age of twenty-five—over her protests—she was made abbess and, except for three years, remained the superior there for the rest of her life. During the time of her administration, the convent became one of the most fervent in all Spain, and she died with a reputation for great holiness. The cause for her canonization was introduced in 1762 by the Congregation of Rites at the request of the Court of Spain.

We should mention a remarkable fact about Mary that bears witness to her visionary gifts: She is the subject of one of the most thoroughly documented cases of bilocation in history. In the 1630s, without ever leaving her convent in Spain, she appeared on numerous occasions to certain native Americans of what is now western Texas, Arizona, and New Mexico.

Mary catechized them in the Catholic faith and instructed them to seek out and be baptized by Franciscan missionaries. The friars were amazed to hear of the natives' encounters with "the Lady in Blue." (The habit of her order, the Conceptionists, was white with a blue cloak.) This miraculous ministry was amply corroborated by witnesses on both sides of the Atlantic: She reported to her sisters in the convent accurate details of the people and places she had encountered in the areas where she had appeared.[12]

Mary is chiefly known, however, for writing a book entitled *The Mystical City of God: A Divine History of the Virgin Mother of God*. Though the text focuses on the life of the Blessed Virgin

---

[11]  E. Graham, "Ven. Marina de Escobar," in *The Catholic Encyclopedia* (New York: Robert Appleton Company, 1909); http://www.newadvent.org/cathen/05534a.htm; J. Verbillion, "Ven. Marina de Escobar," in *The New Catholic Encyclopedia*, vol. 5 (New York: McGraw-Hill, 1967), 538–39.
[12]  Brown, *Life of Mary*, 8.

Mary, her life is of course intimately intertwined with that of Saint Joseph. For this reason, the work devotes considerable time to her visions of Our Lord's foster father.

*The Mystical City* was first conceived nine years after Mary became a nun, but written down ten years later at the command of her confessor. She wrote the first part, consisting of four hundred pages, in only twenty days. Her desire was to keep it from publication, but a copy was sent to the Spanish King Philip IV. Later, in obedience to another confessor, she tossed the book and all her other writings into the flames. Then, in 1655, a third command of her spiritual director caused her to start again. She finished the project in 1670.

*The Mystical City* is presented as a record of special messages from God, received in contemplation and revealed in mysteries, that tell the life of the Virgin Mary. It overflows with elaborate detail, describing both interior and exterior events beginning with the Virgin's conception and extending to her coronation in heaven. As soon as the text found a public beyond Spain, it provoked a fierce storm of controversy.

It is not difficult to see why. Read as a precise theological treatise, a reliable historical account, an accurate scientific text, or even an exact record of what Mary heard and saw in her visions, the book presents numerous problems. She herself had been reluctant to see it published, perhaps thinking that the visions were intended more for her personal reflection than for public dissemination, and that much of what she saw and heard, as she often put it, was "indescribable" in the first place.

Difficulties were compounded by several factors: claims that Mary's confessors had tampered with the text, political tensions between France and Spain, theological debates between the Franciscans (her order) and their philosophical rivals, and certain mistranslations and misinterpretations of the original Spanish by non-native speakers. In general, the book was widely praised and approved in Spain, but condemned elsewhere.[13]

---

[13]   Paul Thigpen, *The Passion: Reflections on the Suffering and Death of Christ* (Charlotte, NC: TAN Books, 2004), xvi–xvii.

In time, however, Mary's mystical work attracted an enthusiastic international following. Servant of God Prosper Guéranger (1805–75), the celebrated abbot of the Benedictine monastery in Solesmes, France, wrote twenty-four articles in defense of the book. He concluded: "The revelations of Mary of Ágreda on the life of the Blessed Virgin have a right to the respect and the esteem of all those who are capable of undertaking to read them . . . they deserve to occupy a distinguished place among writings of that kind, and . . . the judicious use that can be made of them can serve as a powerful stimulus to a revival of devotion in souls."[14]

## Servant of God Maria Baij (1694–1766)

Maria Cecilia Baij was born in 1694 in Montefiascone, an Italian village about sixty miles north of Rome. At the age of twenty, she professed her religious vows with the Benedictine community there, in St. Peter's Convent. In 1743, she was named abbess of the community and remained in that position until her death at the age of seventy-two.

Maria's spiritual life was characterized by many attacks from the Devil. But she also received mystical revelations about the life of Jesus Christ, Saint Joseph, the Holy Family, and Saint John the Baptist. In obedience to her confessor, she wrote these down in extensive manuscripts that are still in the possession of the community she led.

The manuscript of her book *The Life of Saint Joseph* was completed before Baij's death in 1766, but it remained unknown until 1900, when a Benedictine monk named Dom Willibrord van Heteren found it in St. Peter's Convent. He published some excerpts.

In 1920, a local priest, Msgr. Pietro Bergamaschi, became interested in Baij's writings in the convent archive. He presented them to Pope Benedict XV in a private audience on March 17, 1920, during the month of Saint Joseph. The pope urged Bergamaschi to publish them.

---

[14]   Dom Guéranger, "*La Cité Mystique de Dieu*," *L'Univers*, 1859, Dec. 5, 1858.

Unlike the works of Mary of Ágreda and Anne Catherine Emmerich, *The Life of Saint Joseph* presents visions that focus largely on Our Lord's adoptive father, telling his life story in great detail. It has received from the Vatican an imprimatur and *nihil obstat* officially declaring it free from doctrinal and moral error. But as with the works of the other visionaries, it must be read as a kind of sacred drama rather than biographical history, and some of its details differ from those in other accounts.

Fr. Pascal Parente (d. 1971), a theology professor at the Catholic University of America, has summed up the value of her visions in his introduction to the English edition of the book: "The account of St. Joseph's life . . . was not intended essentially to provide exegetical or historical instruction but rather to serve as a means of edification. In this respect it has succeeded marvelously. It reveals the most loving and lovable head of the Holy Family in a new light which cannot fail to impress both the mind and the heart of the reader, thereby making him a partaker of the heavenly peace and harmony that reigned in the Holy Family of Nazareth." Parente deemed Maria's visions "a major contribution to our Catholic heritage of . . . mystical literature."[15]

## *Blessed Anne Catherine Emmerich (1774–1824)*

Anne Catherine Emmerich entered the Augustinian convent of Agnetenberg in Dulmen, Germany, at the age of twenty-eight. Beginning in her childhood, the supernatural realm seemed ordinary to her; she frequently experienced mystical visions and displayed extraordinary gifts. She predicted certain happenings accurately and could hear and see remote events. When the sick came to visit her, though she had no medical training, she could diagnose the causes of their problems and prescribe remedies that worked. Nevertheless, her own physical condition was frail and troublesome.

---

[15]    Courtney Mares, "How a Forgotten Nun's Visions Shed 'New Light' on the Life of St. Joseph," *Catholic News Agency*, March 16, 2021; https://angelusnews.com/faith/how-a-forgotten-nuns-visions-shed-new-light-on-the-life-of-st-joseph/; Maria Cecilia Baij, *The Life of Saint Joseph* (Asbury, NJ: The 101 Foundation, 1997), i–iii.

The sisters in the convent remained suspicious of her because of her unusual powers and poor health, and they were annoyed by her frequent ecstasies. In 1812, the government of Napoleon closed the institution, and Anne Catherine was forced to seek lodging with a poor widow. In 1813, she became bedridden.

Soon after, the stigmata—the wounds of Christ—appeared on her body, including the marks of the thorns. She tried to conceal them, as well as the crosses that appeared on her breast, but word got out, and soon the local bishop sent a commission to examine the unusual phenomena. Though the examination was strict, in the end, the vicar general and three physicians who administered it were thoroughly convinced that the stigmata were genuine.

Some years later, a noted German poet, Clemens Brentano (1778–1842), visited her, was converted, and remained daily at her bedside from 1820 to 1824, taking notes on her visions and mystical experiences as she described them. Each day he would rewrite the notes, replacing her local dialect with standard German, then read them back to her for her revision and approval. Brentano was deeply impressed by her purity, humility, and patience under remarkably intense suffering.

In 1833, some years after the nun's death, Brentano published the compilation of these notes, under the title *The Dolorous Passion of Our Lord Jesus Christ According to the Meditations of Anne Catherine Emmerich*. The book focuses on her visions of His suffering, death, and resurrection. They are remarkable for their vivid detail, their simplicity of style, and the passionate participation of the visionary in the events described.

We cannot be certain how much Brentano may have added in his attempt to organize and clarify the material. For this reason, the Church explicitly declared that these texts would not have any role in the process of her consideration for canonization. (Anne Catherine was declared "Blessed" by the Church in 2004.) Even so, the work reflects brightly the fire and purity of a soul who was consumed by love for her Lord.[16]

---

[16] Thigpen, *Passion*, xvii–xviii.

Archbishop William H. Elder of Cincinnati wrote approvingly of the work in 1892: *"The Life of Our Lord,* according to the revelations of Catherine Emmerich, I have found extremely interesting and edifying. . . . If received according to the explanations given and if read in the spirit of piety, it is wonderfully adapted to increase in our heart the love of Our Lord Jesus Christ, by giving us vivid pictures of what He did and said during His mortal life."[17]

## *A Final Encouragement*

To echo the archbishop's encouragement, I present *The Life of Saint Joseph as Seen by the Mystics* with the hope that these visionaries' powerful insights will increase in your heart a love of Our Lord Jesus Christ, and of all the Holy Family as well. I offer it to my personal patron, Saint Joseph the Worker, as a humble labor of love and with gratitude for his constant care in my life and the life of my family.

At the same time, I recall a few lines from a fascinating apocryphal book of the sixth or seventh century entitled *The History of Joseph the Carpenter.* Perhaps you will forgive me if I dare to hope that the imagined promise made in its pages might at least be possible. In that story, Jesus says to Joseph at the saint's death: "Whoever shall write the history of your life, your labor, and your departure from this world . . . I will commit to your care as long as he remains in this life. And when his soul departs from the body, and when he must leave this world, I will burn the book of his sins; I will not torment him with any punishment in the day of judgment; but he shall cross the sea of flames, and shall go through it without trouble or pain."[18]

THE COMPILER
Solemnity of Saint Joseph, 2022

---

[17]   Quoted in Brown, *Life of Mary,* 17.
[18]   *The History of Joseph the Carpenter,* in *The Ante-Nicene Fathers: Translations of the Fathers Down to a.d. 325,* vol. 3, *Fathers of the Third and Fourth Centuries* (1886; repr., Grand Rapids, MI: William B. Eerdmans, 1986), 392–93.

# CHAPTER ONE

# THE EARLY LIFE OF JOSEPH

JOSEPH'S marvelous holiness began with the formation of his body in the womb of his mother. In this the providence of God Himself intervened, making his body a blessed earth fit for the dwelling of an exquisite soul and well-balanced mind. The holy child was born most beautiful and perfect of body.

Joseph's first words were "My God." That is what his guardian angel had taught him. His parents heard it with amazement. He often renewed this gift of himself to God.

The Lord advanced in Joseph the use of his reason, perfecting it at an early age. He endowed his mind with infused knowledge and enhanced his soul with new graces and virtues. From that time the child began to know God by faith, and also by natural reasoning and science, as the Cause and Author of all things.

After he was able to walk unhampered, little Joseph often went and hid himself in order to pray. With uplifted hands, he would offer thanks to God for all the good things He had given him. His words were still somewhat stammering, but they came from a heart inflamed for God.

In time the child began to see how seriously God was being offended by His creatures. For that reason, he would often cry in grief, but he did it in a way that was hidden from his parents so that they would not be troubled by his tears. By offering these innocent tears, he obtained from God greater graces and illuminations. In return, Joseph would give thanks once more to the most gracious God.

Whenever the little boy was carried around by his mother, and found himself where he could see the open sky, he would gaze firmly up into the heavens. His joy and exultation showed that all his happiness and treasure lay in heaven. As his mother observed this, she would often bring him to a place where he could have an unobstructed view of the sky. She also did it whenever she saw that he was sad, because it would lift his spirits.

In addition to his regular guardian angel, Joseph had another angel assigned to him by God. This guardian spoke to him often in his dreams and was given to Joseph to instruct him in all those things that would be required of him. In this way he could become ever-more pleasing to God.

Joseph's parents and his angel told him about the coming of the Messiah. So he sent fervent appeals to God, asking Him to grant that the time of waiting would be shortened. From that time on, he applied all his prayers to this intention.

The young boy eagerly listened to and understood profoundly all that was taught him in regard to God and His works. At a precocious age he already practiced the highest kinds of prayer and contemplation and eagerly engaged in the exercise of the virtues proper to his youth. At the time when others come to the use of reason (at the age of seven years or more), Joseph was already a perfect man in the use of it and in holiness. He was of a kind disposition, loving, affable, sincere, showing inclinations not just holy but angelic, growing in virtue and perfection and advancing toward an altogether irreproachable life.

Joseph always undertook any task that he knew would please God. Among other gifts, he had received a special talent for giving effective assistance to the afflicted. Whenever he talked with them, his attitude and behavior always managed to alleviate their sorrow.

Of course, he always turned to God and pled fervently for comfort on behalf of those he was assisting. His ability to ease the burden of the oppressed became known throughout the town and brought many to his home to listen to him and receive his help.

The Lord gave young Joseph a special concern for the poor who were dying. He realized that Satan would make every effort to conquer a soul and lead it into eternal misery. His angel had once told him about the great danger faced by the dying; after that, God inspired his heart with a great sympathy and fervent love for them.

Joseph came to their aid with deep concern. The Lord intended that he would be the patron saint of the dying, so He wanted him to begin even in this life such a great work of love. He enabled Joseph to discern the needs of various souls in their last moments. Knowing that the hour of death determines for every soul an eternity of either unceasing happiness or perpetual misery, Joseph had an urgent desire to assist these souls.

Whenever anything took place in Joseph's home that would offend God—this sometimes happened among the servants through moral weakness—the young boy would grow sad and sorrowful. At such a young age, he could not take them to task. But he would demonstrate his displeasure at their sins by crying.

Satan was aware of the light that dwelt in young Joseph. He feared that this child would stir up others to engage in battle with him, and by his example lead many souls toward a life of devotion. He attempted many times to take Joseph's life, but his plotting was always thwarted, because the child was protected by the all-powerful arm of God.

Just the sight of such a virtuous child enraged the Devil. Once, he pushed the boy headlong down a flight of stairs. The Lord allowed such an attack to allow Joseph a chance to practice virtue and to humiliate the Enemy. As he was falling, the child cried to God for help, who protected him from harm. While Satan was forced to withdraw in confusion, Joseph received another opportunity to give thanks and praise to God for His care.

Joseph was protected by the two angels who had been assigned as his guardians. Though the Enemy raged with fury, he could not carry out his plans. He tried to stir up strife and confusion between the boy's parents. He even tried to attack others in the household. But every time, he failed.

In every such situation, Joseph prayed, and God heard his prayers. Often he would join fasting to his petitions, and the Devil was deprived of his might. He always found himself conquered and beaten, because Joseph's prayers had great power.

The angel who had been assigned to speak to Joseph when he dreamed always counseled him about what he must do to overcome the infernal spirit. As soon as the Devil began to prepare to mount another attack on the household, the guardian would let Joseph know, and the young saint never failed to heed the angel's warning.

Joseph's parents lived in a large mansion outside of Bethlehem. It was the ancient birthplace of David, whose father Jesse had owned it. But by Joseph's time only the main walls were still in existence as part of the structure. He was the third of six brothers; three of them were his natural brothers and two were his stepbrothers.

In front of the house was a large courtyard with a garden. In it was a stone house built over a spring whose waters gushed forth out of faucets, each of which was crafted to represent some animal's head. The garden was enclosed by walls like a cloister and surrounded by colonnades with sculptures like the heads of men. Alongside the colonnades were trees and shrubbery. The lower story of the dwelling had a door, but no windows.

In the upper story there were circular openings. Over these there ran, around the whole top of the house, a broad gallery with four little pavilions capped by cupolas. From these cupolas, a view far into the surrounding country was possible.

Above the center of the flat roof arose another, smaller story, also crowned by a tower and cupola. Joseph and his brothers occupied that last story with an aged Jewish man, their tutor. The tutor lived in the highest room in the story, while the brothers slept in one chamber, their sleeping places separated from one another by mats, which in the daytime were rolled up against the walls.

They often played up there, each in his own separate space. They had toys shaped like little animals. Their tutor gave them all sorts of unusual lessons, including lessons in measurement.

The father and mother of the boys were neither good nor bad. They did not trouble themselves much about their children; they paid very little attention to them. When they were absent, Joseph's brothers used to play all kinds of tricks on him and knock him around.

The brothers were mean to him because they recognized that Joseph was quite different from them. He was very gifted and he learned quickly. But he was simple in his tastes, quiet, devout, and not at all ambitious.

The boys all had separate little gardens where they grew herbs, bushes, and small trees. Joseph's brothers would often sneak into his garden to trample and uproot the plants there. They always treated him roughly, but he bore everything patiently.

Sometimes, when Joseph was kneeling in prayer in the colonnade that ran around the courtyard, with his face turned to the wall, his brothers would push him over. Once, when he was praying this way, one of the brothers kicked him in the back, but Joseph appeared not to notice it. The other child repeated his blows with such violence that at last Joseph fell forward onto the hard, cold floor.

Joseph, however, had not been in a waking condition, but in an ecstasy of prayer. When he came to himself, he did not lose his temper or seek to take revenge. He merely turned away quietly and sought another secluded spot.

Joseph's parents were not well satisfied with him. They wanted him, on account of his talents, to fit himself for a position in the world. But he had no desire for that. He was too simple and unpretentious for them. His only inclination was toward prayer and quiet work at some handicraft.

At about the age of twelve, he often went beyond Bethlehem to escape the harassment of his brothers. Not far from the cave that would one day hold the crib of Jesus, there was a little community of some very pious, old Jewish women. Joseph often went to them in his troubles and shared their devotions.

Sometimes he spent time in their neighborhood with a master carpenter, lending him a helping hand. The carpenter taught him his trade, and Joseph found the lessons in measurement he had learned from his tutor to be of use in that work.

The hostility of his brothers at last went so far that, when he was eighteen, Joseph could no longer remain in his parents' home. So he fled the house by night. A friend, who lived outside of Bethlehem, had brought him clothes in which to make his escape.

Joseph settled at first in a small village, carrying on carpentry. He worked for his living in a very poor family. The father of the family supported himself by making the kind of rough wicker partitions that Joseph knew how to put together. The saint humbly assisted the family as much as he could. He gathered wood and carried it to the house.

Joseph's parents, in the meantime, believed that he had been kidnapped. But his brothers found him out, and then he was again persecuted. Yet Joseph would not leave the poor family nor stop practicing the humble occupation of which his own family was ashamed. Wherever he lived, he was always loved by those who knew him. He was a good, kind, and devout workingman—lovable, gentle, and utterly sincere.

Later, Joseph moved again to another village. There, he did better work for a well-to-do family, and the carpenter's work which they did was of higher quality. Though a small place, the village had a synagogue. At last he worked for a master carpenter in Tiberias, where he lived alone near the water.

By that time, Joseph's parents had died, and his brothers had scattered. Only two of them still dwelled in Bethlehem. His father's mansion had passed into other hands, and the whole family had rapidly declined.

Now a grown man, Joseph remained deeply pious. He prayed fervently for the coming of the Messiah. He showed great reserve in the presence of females. From the age of twelve he had made and perfectly kept a vow of chastity, and his purity of soul, which was known to all, was that of an angel.

The saint was so reserved and careful in his speech that not one word ever issued from his mouth that was not good and holy, nor did he ever indulge in unnecessary or less than charitable conversation. He was most patient and diligent in bearing fatigue; he practiced extreme poverty; he was most meek in bearing injuries; he was strong and constant against enemies; and he was the faithful witness of the wonders of heaven.

# CHAPTER TWO

# THE WEDDING AND THE EARLY DAYS IN NAZARETH

ONE day Joseph entertained the idea of fitting up a more secluded place of prayer in his dwelling. But an angel appeared to him in prayer and told him not to do it: For just as in ancient times the Old Testament patriarch Joseph became, by God's appointment, the administrator of the Egyptian granaries, so now to this Joseph was the granary of Redemption to be wedded. In his humility Joseph could not comprehend the meaning of this message, so he gave himself to prayer about it.

Meanwhile, Mary and seven other virgins who had, as young girls, been presented for service in the Temple, were now to be dismissed from there and given in marriage. For this reason, Mary's mother, Anne, went to Jerusalem to be with her. The young woman grieved at the thought of leaving the Temple, for she had made before God a private vow to perpetual chastity. But she was told that she must be married.

Then the Lord appeared to Mary and said to her: "My spouse and my dove, let your troubled heart be lifted up; do not let it be disturbed or sad. I will listen to your desires and to your requests; I will direct all things, and I will guide the priests by enlightening them.

"I will give you a spouse that I Myself have selected, one who will place no obstacle to your holy desires; instead, by my grace he will support you in them. I will find for you a perfect man who fulfills My will, and I will choose him from the number of My servants. My power is infinite, and My protection and aid will never fail you."

At the Temple, one of the distinguished old priests, who was no longer able to walk, was carried into the Holy of Holies. An incense offering was kindled. The priest prayed as he sat before a scroll of Scripture, and in a vision his hand was placed upon a verse about the Messiah in the prophet Isaiah: "There shall come forth a rod out of the root of Jesse, and a flower shall rise up out of his root" [see Is 11:1].

Then all the unmarried men in the country of the House of David (except for Joseph) were summoned to the Temple. Many of them made their appearance in holiday attire. Mary was conducted into their presence. It was her fourteenth birthday.

One among them was a very pious youth from the region of Bethlehem, who had always ardently prayed to be allowed to serve the advent of the Messiah. His desire to wed Mary was great. Mary, however, wept; she had no desire to take a husband.

The high priest, according to the inward instructions he had received, gave to each of the suitors a branch. He instructed each man to inscribe his name on his branch and to hold it in his hand during the offering of prayer and sacrifice. After that, all the branches were laid on an altar in the Holy of Holies of the Temple with the understanding that the one whose branch should blossom was to be Mary's husband. Knowing that she was an unusually beautiful and virtuous maiden with a good inheritance, they were eager to win her hand.

Now when that youth who so ardently desired to wed Mary found that his branch, along with all the others, had failed to blossom, he withdrew to a hall outside the Temple. With his arms raised to God, he wept bitterly. The other suitors left the Temple. That youth hurried to Mount Carmel where, since the days of Elijah, hermits had lived. He made the mount his dwelling, and there he spent his days in prayer for the coming of the Messiah.

Once the men were sent home, the priests hunted through various scrolls in their search for another descendant of the House of David, one who had not presented himself among the suitors for Mary's hand. There they found that, among the six brothers of Bethlehem, one was unknown and ignored. They sought him out.

They found Joseph at last and told him to go up to the Temple. So he went right away, arrayed in his best. A branch was given to him. As he was about to lay it upon the altar, it blossomed on top into a white flower like a lily.

At the same time a light from the Holy Spirit hovered over him. A dove of the purest and most dazzling white was seen to descend and rest on his head for a moment. Then God said in the saint's heart: "Joseph, My servant, Mary shall be your spouse. Receive her with all care and respect, for she is pleasing in My sight. She is righteous and pure in mind and body. And you shall perform all that she shall ask."

When Mary appeared, calm and beautiful and humbly resigned to God's will, the priests betrothed her to the most chaste and holy of men, Joseph. Then, according to the Jewish custom, the two parted until the wedding.

The touching wedding ceremony took place later in a rented house on Mount Zion in Jerusalem near the Temple. Besides Mary's teachers and friends from the Temple, the guests included some relatives of her parents, who had prepared for her a lovely sky-blue wedding gown and cape, though in her humility she hesitated to accept it. Joseph wore a plain, long, gray robe.

After the wedding, Mary sadly took leave of the priests and her teachers and companions, thanking them all for their kindness to her during her years among them. And then, offering up her own desire to remain in the Lord's house all her life, with keen grief she left the Temple. In the company of Joseph and some attendants sent by the priests, she set out, with perfect resignation and trust in God, for the new life to which He was leading her in Nazareth.

The seven virgins that were to leave the Temple with Mary had already departed. They were recalled to accompany Mary on her festal journey to Nazareth, where her mother Anne had already prepared their little home.

The marriage feast lasted a week. The women and the virgins, companions of Mary in the Temple, were present, as well as many relatives of Mary's parents Joachim and Anne, and two daughters from another village. Many lambs were slaughtered and offered in sacrifice.

The very wealthy among the Jews in attendance changed their clothes three or four times during the marriage feast, as was their custom. Mary was dressed in magnificent apparel, presenting an appearance somewhat similar to the richly adorned women of a much later period. The usual clothing of the Jewish women of that day wrapped closely around them, but Mary's wedding dress was very different; it was something of the Roman style.

Joseph wore a long, wide, blue coat fastened from the breast down with loops and buttons. The wide sleeves were laced at the sides, a broad cuff turned up at the wrist, the inside provided with pockets. Around the neck was something like a brown collar, over which lay a kind of stole, and upon the breast hung two white bands.

After the marriage feast, Joseph went to Bethlehem on some business, and Mary with twelve or fifteen women and maidens went to Anne's house near Nazareth. They made the journey on foot. When Joseph returned, there was at Anne's house a feast at which, besides the usual household, there were about six adult guests and several children present.

Joseph and Mary settled into their house near Nazareth. Both were at first timid and reserved in each other's presence. They were very quiet and prayerful.

In this home, Mary and Joseph had, properly speaking, no regular housekeeping affairs; they received from Anne all that they needed. Mary would spin, sew, and embroider, and the cooking she did was very simple, eating mostly bread and sheep's milk; the only meat they ate was pigeons.

This little house at Nazareth that Anne fitted up for Mary and Joseph belonged to Anne. From her own dwelling, she could, unnoticed, reach it in about half an hour by a cross path. It lay not far from the city gate.

It had a small courtyard in front, and nearby was a well, with a couple of steps leading down to it. It was near a hill, but not built on it. Joseph had his own sleeping compartment. Mary's sleeping compartment was in the back, and there it was that the angelic Annunciation took place.

At their home in Nazareth, Mary and Joseph were welcomed and visited by their friends and relatives with the joyful congratulations customarily offered at such times. After they had in a most holy way fulfilled the natural duties of friendship and politeness, and satisfied the worldly obligations connected with conversation and interaction with others, the two most holy spouses were left at leisure and to their own counsel in their house. A custom among the Jews required that for the first few days of their married state, the husband and wife should enter upon a sort of study of each other's habits and temperament, so that afterwards they might be able to make a mutual allowance for what they observed in their conduct with each other.

During this time Joseph said to Mary: "My spouse and Lady, I give thanks to the Lord, the Most High God, for the favor of having designated me as your husband, despite my lack of merits, though I judged myself unworthy even of your company. But His Majesty, who can raise up the lowly whenever He wishes, showed this mercy to me, and I desire and hope, relying on your discretion and virtue, that you will help me make a proper return in serving Him with an upright heart.

"Keep me, then, as your servant, and by the true love which I have for you, I beg you to make up for my deficiencies in the fulfillment of domestic duties and of other things that, as a worthy husband, I should know how to perform. Tell me, Lady, what is your pleasure, so that I may fulfill it."

Mary heard these words with a humble heart, and yet also with a serene earnestness, and she answered Joseph: "My master, I am fortunate that the Most High, in order to place me in this state of life, has chosen you for my husband, and that He has given me such an obvious revelation of His will that I should serve you. But if you give me permission, I will speak of my thoughts and intentions, which I want to reveal to you for this purpose."

God strengthened the sincere and upright heart of Joseph with His grace and kindled it anew with divine love through the word of most holy Mary. He answered her: "Speak, Lady, your servant is listening."

On this occasion the mistress of the world was surrounded by the thousand angels of her guard, in a form visible only to her. She had a natural shyness and anxiety that she always felt in speaking to men alone; she had never done this, except perhaps unintentionally with the high priest. So the holy angels obeyed their Queen and stood in attendance, to remind her that she was not alone.

In this glorious company she spoke to Joseph: "My lord and spouse, it is right for us to give praise and glory with all reverence to our God and Creator, who is infinite in goodness and incomprehensible in His judgments. To us, who are so needy, He has manifested His greatness and mercy in choosing us for His service.

"I acknowledge myself among all creatures to be more obliged and indebted to Him than all others, and more than all of them together. For, though meriting less, I have received from His generous hand more than they. At a young age I was convinced to consecrate myself to God through a perpetual vow of chastity in body and soul by the force of this truth which, with the knowledge of the deceitfulness of visible things, His divine light made known to me. I am His, and I acknowledge Him as my Spouse and Lord, with a firm resolve to preserve for Him my chastity.

"I beg you, my master, to help me in fulfilling this vow. Meanwhile, in all other things I will be your servant, willing to work for the comfort of your life as long as mine shall last. Yield, my spouse, to this resolution and make a similar one so that, offering ourselves as an acceptable sacrifice to our eternal God, He may receive us in the fragrance of sweetness and grant us the eternal goods for which we hope."

The most chaste spouse Joseph, full of interior joy at the words of his heavenly spouse, answered her: "My mistress, in making known to me your chaste and welcome intentions, you have penetrated and enlarged my heart. I did not reveal my own thoughts to you before knowing yours.

"I also acknowledge myself under greater obligation to the Lord of creation than other men; for very early He has called me by His true enlightenment to love Him with an upright heart. I want you to know, Lady, that at the age of twelve years I also made a promise to serve the Most High in perpetual chastity.

"On this account I now gladly ratify this vow in order not to impede your own. In the presence of His Majesty, I promise to aid you, as far as in me lies, in serving Him and loving Him according to your full desires. I will be, by God's grace, your most faithful servant and companion, and I ask you to accept my chaste love and hold me as your brother, without ever entertaining any other kind of love besides the one which you owe to God, and after God, to me."

In this conversation the Most High confirmed anew the virtue of chastity in the heart of Joseph, and the pure and holy love due to his most holy spouse, Mary. This love the saint already had to an eminent degree, and the Lady herself increased it sweetly, enlarging his heart by her most wise conversation.

Through God's action, the two holy and chaste spouses felt an incomparable joy and consolation. The heavenly princess, as one who is the mistress of all virtues and who in all things pursued the highest perfection of all virtues, lovingly corresponded to the desires of Joseph. The Most High also gave to Joseph new purity and a complete command over his natural inclinations. In that way, he could without hindrance or any trace of sensual desires, but with admirable and new grace, serve Mary, and in her, carry out God's will and pleasure.

As we have seen, in his earlier life Joseph had learned the trade of carpentry as a respectable and proper way of earning a living. He was poor in earthly possessions, and it was necessary to do some work and not to remain idle. So he asked Mary whether she would find it agreeable for him to exercise his trade in order to be able to serve her and to gain something for distribution among the poor. The most prudent Virgin approved of this intention, saying that the Lord did not wish them to be rich, but poor and lovers of the poor, seeking to help them as far as their means would allow.

Then there arose between the two spouses a holy contest about who should obey the other as superior. But she, who among the humble was the most humble, won in this contest of humility. For as the man is the head of the family, she would not permit this natural order to be inverted. She desired in all things to obey her spouse Joseph, asking him only for permission to help the poor, which the saint gladly gave.

During these days, by divine enlightenment Joseph learned to know more and more the qualities of his spouse. Her rare prudence, humility, purity, and all her other virtues exceeded by far his thoughts and estimates. He was seized with ever-new admiration, and in great joy of spirit he continued to praise and thank the Lord again and again for having given him a companion and spouse so far above his merits.

God ordained that the princess of heaven, by her mere presence and conversation, should infuse into the heart of her spouse a holy fear and reverence greater than words could ever describe. This effect was worked on Joseph by a radiant splendor reflecting the divine light, shining from the face of our Queen and mingled with an inexpressible and always visible majesty. Such radiance was more merited than the radiance of Moses's face had been merited when he descended from the mountain [Ex 24:30], for her dealings and conversation with God had been even more extended and intimate than his.

In this way the Most High began the greatest work that He was ever to carry out by His omnipotence, a work of utter perfection.

# CHAPTER THREE

## *THE ANNUNCIATION AND THE VISITATION*

ONE day, a short time after the wedding, the Blessed Virgin was at home alone in the house of Nazareth. Joseph was at that time journeying with two beasts of burden on the road to Tiberias, where he was going to get his tools. But Anne was in the house with her maid and two of the virgins who had been with Mary in the Temple.

After Mary went to her room to pray, the Archangel Gabriel appeared to her just as we read in the Gospel, and she gave her consent to God's plan. When the angel and the streams of glory accompanying him vanished, a path of light led up to heaven, with showers of half-opened roses and tiny green leaves falling upon Mary. Entirely absorbed in what had happened, she saw in herself the Incarnate Son of God, a tiny, human form of light with all the members, even the little fingers perfect. It was about midnight.

After the Annunciation, when Jesus had been conceived, Joseph returned from Tiberias. At that time the Blessed Virgin experienced a great desire to visit her cousin Elizabeth. Joseph, even though he had not yet fully settled at Nazareth, started on the journey with Mary to Zachariah and Elizabeth's house in Hebron, to the south.

Their destination was more than eighty miles distant from Nazareth. The greater part of the way was very rough and broken, unfit for such a delicate and tender maiden. The only convenience at their disposal for the arduous undertaking was a donkey, on which she began and continued her journey.

Although the humble beast was intended solely for her comfort and service, yet Mary, the most humble and unpretentious of all creatures, many times dismounted and asked Joseph to share with her this convenience and to lighten the difficulties of the way by riding instead of walking. Her discreet spouse never accepted this offer. But in order to yield somewhat to the solicitations of the heavenly Lady, he permitted her now and then to walk with him part of the way, whenever it seemed to him that her delicate strength could sustain the exertion without excessive fatigue.

Soon, however, he would again ask her, with great modesty and reverence, to accept this slight alleviation of her discomfort. The celestial Queen would then obey and again proceed on her way seated in the saddle. In this way, lessening their fatigue by humbly and courteously taking turns, the most holy Mary and Joseph continued on their journey, making good use of each single moment.

They proceeded alone, with no other people accompanying them. But a thousand angels attended upon them. Although the angels who accompanied them appeared in bodily form— serving their great Queen and her most holy Son in her womb—they were visible only to Mary.

In the company of the angels and of Joseph, the mother of grace journeyed along, filling the fields and the mountains with the sweetest fragrance of her presence and with the divine praises, which she sang unceasingly. Sometimes she conversed with the angels, and at other times she sang with them divine canticles about the various mysteries of God and the works of creation and the Incarnation. In this way, the pure heart of the immaculate Lady was inflamed ever anew by the fervor of divine love.

In all this, Joseph contributed his share by maintaining a discreet silence, and by allowing his beloved spouse to pursue the flights of her spirit. Lost in highest contemplation, he was favored with some understanding of what was passing within her soul. At other times the two would converse with each other about the salvation of souls and the mercies of the Lord, of the coming of the Redeemer, of the prophecies given to the ancient Fathers concerning Him, and of other mysteries and sacraments of the Most High.

Something happened on the way that caused great wonder in Joseph: He loved his spouse most tenderly with a chaste and holy love, which had been ordained in him by the special grace and dispensation of the divine Love itself. In addition to this privilege (which was certainly not a small one), the saint was naturally of a most noble and courteous disposition, and his manners were most pleasing and charming.

All this produced in him a most discreet and loving attentiveness, which was increased by the great holiness that he had seen from the beginning in his spouse, ordained by heaven as the immediate reason for all his privileges. For this reason, the saint eagerly attended to Mary, asking her many times whether she was tired or weary, and in what ways he could serve her on the journey.

Since the Queen of Heaven already carried within her virginal womb the divine fire of the Incarnate Word, holy Joseph, without understanding the real cause, experienced in his soul new effects resulting from the words and conversations of his beloved spouse. He felt himself so inflamed by divine love and imbued with such exalted knowledge of the mysteries touched on in their conversations that he was entirely renewed and spiritualized by this burning interior light.

The farther they proceeded and the more they conversed about these heavenly things, the stronger these affections grew. He became aware that it was the words of his spouse that thus filled his heart with love and inflamed his will with divine fervor.

Having continued their journey four days, holy Mary and her spouse arrived at the town where Zachary and Elizabeth then lived. To announce their visit, Joseph hurried ahead of Mary and called out to them: "The Lord be with you and fill your souls with divine grace."

Elizabeth was already alerted to their arrival, for the Lord Himself had informed her in a vision that Mary of Nazareth had left home to visit her. She had also in this vision been made aware that the heavenly Lady was most pleasing in the eyes of the Most High (though the mystery of her being the Mother of God was not revealed to her until the moment when they both saluted each other in private). Elizabeth immediately came outside with a few of her family members to welcome Mary.

As the humbler and younger woman, Mary hurried to greet her cousin, saying, "The Lord be with you, my dearest cousin."

Elizabeth answered: "The same Lord reward you for having come in order to afford me this pleasure." When the cousins met, they greeted each other joyfully with outstretched hands. There was a light in Mary, and a ray of it shone out from her and entered into Elizabeth, who was marvelously stirred up by it. They did not pause long, but arm in arm walked through the courtyard to the door of the house, where Elizabeth once more welcomed Mary.

Joseph went around to the side of the house and into an open hall where Zachariah sat. He respectfully greeted the aged priest, who responded in writing on his tablet, since he was unable to speak until John the Baptist was born. Meanwhile, Mary and Elizabeth entered a room with a fireplace. Here they embraced, clasping each other in their arms and pressing cheek to cheek. Light was streaming down between them.

At that moment Elizabeth, becoming inflamed within, stepped back with uplifted hands and exclaimed, "Blessed are you among women, and blessed is the Fruit of your womb!" [Lk 1:42]. Then she continued to speak just as we read her words in the Gospel, with Mary's reply as also found there.

Joseph and Zachariah were conversing by means of the tablet, and always about the coming of the Messiah. Zachariah was a tall, handsome, old man clothed like a priest. He and Joseph sat together at the side of the house that opened on the garden, in which Mary and Elizabeth were now sitting on a rug under a high, spreading tree.

Behind the tree was a fountain from which gushed water when a faucet was opened. Grass and flowers were all around, and trees bearing little yellow plums. Mary and Elizabeth were eating rolls and small fruits out of Joseph's travelling pouch, with touching simplicity and moderation. Two men and two women servants were in the house; they prepared a table under the tree. Joseph and Zachariah came out and had something to eat.

Joseph wanted to return home at once, but they persuaded him to stay eight days. He knew nothing of Mary's conception. The women were silent on that subject. They had a secret understanding together about their interior feelings.

When all of them—Mary and Elizabeth, Joseph and Zachariah—were together, they prayed, making use of a kind of litany. In the evening they all sat together again in the garden near a lamp under the tree. A cover like a tent was stretched under the tree, and low stools with backs stood around. After that, Joseph and Zachariah went into a prayer room, and Mary and Elizabeth withdrew to their little chamber to pray.

Over the following days, the two couples spent their time together in prayer and in holy conversation. When the Sabbath arrived, it was celebrated in a room in Zachariah's house with lighted lamps. Zachariah, Joseph, and about six other men from the neighborhood were standing and praying under one of the lamps and around a little chest on which lay scrolls of writing. They had on their heads something like a small veil, and they frequently bowed their heads and raised their arms as they prayed.

Mary, Elizabeth, and two other women stood apart in a grated partition from which they could see into the place of prayer. They were entirely wrapped up, with their prayer cloaks over their heads. When the Sabbath was over, they took their meal together under the trees in the garden near the house.

Joseph had asked permission of his heavenly spouse to return to Nazareth and leave her in the company of Elizabeth to assist her in her pregnancy. He left them with the understanding that he was to return to accompany Mary home as soon as they would give him notice.

Elizabeth offered him some gifts to take home with him, but he would take only a few of them, finally yielding to her earnest entreaties. For this man of God was not only a lover of poverty, but he also possessed a magnanimous and noble heart. With these he prepared to return to Nazareth, taking along with him the little beast of burden that they had brought with them.

After the meal, Joseph, accompanied by Zachariah, started on his journey home. Before they left, they embraced Mary and Elizabeth, alternately pressing them to their heart, but without kissing. Then each one prayed.

Their parting was calm and cheerful. The two women accompanied them a short distance, and then the travelers proceeded alone. The night was unspeakably lovely: calm, with the moon shining and the sky studded with stars.

Joseph took with him his little bundle, with a few of the rolls and a small jug of something to drink. Both the travelers had a staff, but Joseph's was hooked on top, while Zachariah's was long and ended in a knob. Both had traveling cloaks that they wore over their head.

After they had travelled a distance, they spent the night in a shed. On the rest of their journey, they took very winding roads and visited many people, for it was three days before Zachariah returned home and Joseph arrived back in Nazareth. Anne's maid took charge of the house for Joseph, going back and forth between the two homes. With this exception, he was entirely alone.

The Blessed Virgin remained with Elizabeth three months, until after the birth of John. But she returned to Nazareth before his circumcision.

# CHAPTER FOUR

## *JOSEPH LEARNS OF MARY'S CHILD*

NOW that the Blessed Virgin was in her fifth month of pregnancy, one day when Joseph saw her coming out of her place of prayer, he could not help noticing the evident change in her condition, which she never tried to conceal. But he was completely unable to explain what he saw so clearly. Naturally, because he loved his dear wife so tenderly, he felt a keen stab of grief in his heart.

The consternation Joseph felt was one of the heaviest crosses he ever had to bear. Even so, since he was a holy and just man, he withheld his judgment. But he began to worry over the matter more and more.

Joseph dreaded the terrible thought that he might be forced to give Mary over to the authorities to be stoned, according to the Law of Moses. But he did not dare to speak to her about this delicate subject, since she did not volunteer any information. Instead, he turned to the Lord in frequent, fervent prayers, saying: "Most High God, my grief is almost killing me! My reason declares her blameless, while my senses accuse her. What shall I do? Why does she conceal this matter from me? Yet I will withhold my judgment.

"Receive my tears as an acceptable sacrifice. I do not believe that Mary has offended You. Rule over my mind and my heart."

Meanwhile, Joseph's suffering was known to Mary, and it filled her affectionate heart with intense compassion for him. But she felt obliged to keep God's great secret to herself until He gave her permission to reveal it to anyone. With deep wisdom and confidence, she resigned the whole matter into the hands of Divine Providence.

Mary sought to comfort her good husband in his trouble by attending to him with still more devotion and thoughtfulness. She served him at table, offered him a chair, and often knelt before him. All the time, with the Word Incarnate in her womb, she was growing in health, gracefulness, and loveliness.

Joseph, on the contrary, was so troubled in mind and heart that he was wasting away from weakness and emaciation. Mary spoke to him anxiously about his health and urged him to take some rest and recreation. In great sorrow she prayed fervently to the Lord to console her unhappy husband.

After bearing his tribulation patiently and nobly for two months, Joseph finally came to the sad conclusion that the best thing for him to do was to leave. He decided to depart from his home that very night at midnight.

After packing some clothes in a bundle, he prayed to God: "O Lord, I find no other way to restore my peace. I do not believe my wife is an adulteress. So I will withdraw from her and pass my life in a desert. Do not forsake me, my Lord!" And prostrating himself on the ground, he made a vow to go to the Temple in Jerusalem and offer up a sacrifice so that God might help and protect Mary. Then he took a brief rest.

Meanwhile, Mary, knowing what he was planning to do, also prayed to God: "I beg You, Lord, do not permit him to carry out this decision and leave me!"

The Lord answered her: "My dearest dove, I shall right away visit My servant Joseph with consolation. And after I have revealed to him by My angel the mystery that is now unknown to him, you may tell him openly about all I have done with you. I will fill him with My Spirit, and he will assist you in all that will happen." This divine promise greatly relieved Mary.

Now the Lord mercifully sent the Archangel Gabriel to Joseph while he slept. Though Joseph did not see the angel, he distinctly heard the inner voice say to him: "Do not be afraid, Joseph, son of David, to take Mary, your wife. For the One begotten in her is of the Holy Spirit. And she shall bring forth a Son, and you will call His name Jesus. For He will save His people from their sins" [Mt 1:20–21].

Understanding this great mystery for the first time, Joseph awoke with the overwhelming realization that his wife, Mary, was actually the mother of the Messiah. He was filled with joy and at the same time with sorrow for having doubted her. Prostrating himself on the floor, he humbly gave thanks to God for having revealed this mystery to him.

Then he began to blame himself for all that had happened, exclaiming: "O my heavenly wife, how could your unworthy slave have dared to doubt your faithfulness? How is it that I have not kissed the ground that your feet touched?

"Woe is me—all my thoughts were open to her sight—even that I intended to leave her! O my Lord and God, give me strength to ask her forgiveness, so that for her sake You may pardon my great fault!"

Then, shedding tears of repentance, Joseph unwrapped his bundle, went out of his room, and began to scrub the floors on which Mary walked and to do other chores that he had formerly left to her. For he resolved to be her servant in all things from now on.

Early that morning when he knew that Mary had finished her first prayers and meditation, he went to her room and threw himself on his knees before her with the deepest reverence, saying: "My spouse, Mother of the Eternal Word, I beg you to pardon my audacity. I am certain that none of my thoughts are hidden to your heavenly insight. My presumption was great in deciding to leave you instead of serving you as the mother of my Lord.

"But you know that I did it all in ignorance. Now I consecrate my heart and my whole life to your service. I will not rise from my knees until I have obtained your pardon and your blessing."

Raising him to his feet, Mary knelt before him and said with tender joy and love: "My master and my husband, I should ask you to forgive me for the sorrow and bitterness that I have caused you. As much as I wanted to, I could not on my own account give you any information about the holy Mystery hidden within me by the power of the Almighty.

"But I will always be your faithful servant. The Lord has not made me His mother so that I may be served in this life, but so that I may be the servant of all and your slave. That is my duty."

As Joseph raised her from her knees, the pure and humble Mother of God was filled with the Holy Spirit. All aflame and transfigured in a mystical ecstasy, she recited the *Magnificat.* Seeing her surrounded by a bright radiance of heavenly light, Joseph with profound humility and reverence bowed his head and adored his Lord in her womb. And the Lord looked upon good Joseph with kindly favor and accepted him as His adoptive father, filling his pure heart with holy graces.

After learning that Mary was the chosen Mother of God, Joseph was changed spiritually into a new man. He resolved to act toward her from then on with much greater reverence. Whenever he passed her or spoke to her alone, he respectfully genuflected, and he would no longer let her serve him or clean the house or wash the dishes.

Since she protested, he did these chores during the time she spent in contemplation. Then in her humility, Mary appealed to the Lord, and Joseph's guardian angel was sent to tell him: "Exteriorly allow her to serve you, and interiorly treat her with the highest reverence. Always worship in her the Lord of all creation. It is His will and His mother's to serve and not to be served, to teach the world the value of humility."

In Mary's room was a bed that Joseph had made. When he came to talk with her in her room, he often found her in ecstasy raised above the ground, or conversing with her angels, or prostrate on the floor in the form of a cross. At such times he heard heavenly melodies and noticed a marvelous fragrance, which filled him with deep spiritual joy.

Joseph and Mary now frequently read and discussed together the various prophecies in Holy Scripture concerning the Messiah, especially all that related to His birth. But out of consideration for her husband, the Blessed Virgin did not dwell on the Redeemer's sufferings and death, which had been revealed to her by God. Often during these conversations, Joseph would become so moved by Mary's inspiring words that with tears of joy in his eyes he would exclaim: "Is it really possible that I shall see my God in your arms, and hear Him speak, and touch Him—that He will live with us—that we shall eat at the same table with Him and talk with Him? I do not deserve this good fortune, which no one can ever deserve! Oh, how I regret that I am so poor!"

Then Mary answered: "My master and husband, the Lord is coming to redeem the world and to guide men on the path to life eternal, and this is to be done by means of humility and poverty. In humility and poverty He wishes to be born, to live, and to die, in order to break the chains of greed and pride in human hearts. That is why He chose our poor and humble home and did not want us to be rich in goods that will pass away, which are only vanity and which darken the understanding."

When Joseph asked Mary to instruct him in the various virtues and in the love of God, she did so with touching humility and skill, often by putting questions to him that of themselves suggested the right answers. She also taught him how to make his daily labor more a practice of virtue than mere manual work.

Although both Joseph and Mary performed work for others, they never demanded any wages or set a price on their labor. As they worked not for gain but for charity or to supply a need, they left the payment to their employers and accepted it as freely given alms rather than an earned reward. Joseph learned this perfect degree of sanctity in economic matters from Mary.

Several times during this period they found themselves so poor that they even lacked necessities, for they were extremely generous in their gifts to the needy and they never stocked up food or clothing for the future. In her faith and humility, Mary blessed the Lord for this poverty, which was a source of profound spiritual consolation to her. But she asked God to supply Joseph's needs, and the Lord heard her prayers.

Sometimes He moved their neighbors to bring them gifts or to pay off a debt. At other times Elizabeth sent them presents, which Mary always acknowledged by sending in return some work of her hands. On rare occasions she commanded her friends, the birds, to bring some fish or fruit or bread, and Joseph marveled when he saw the birds come down and place this food in her hands.

One day it happened that they had nothing at all to eat at mealtime. So Mary and Joseph each retired to their room and persevered in prayer, thanking the Lord for this privation and begging Him for help. Meanwhile, angels prepared the table and set on it fresh white bread and fish and fruit, and a wonderfully sweet and nourishing jelly. When they called the holy couple to this truly heaven-sent meal, the Blessed Virgin and her husband wept tears of humble gratitude while they sang hymns of praise and thanks to God.

As Mary's pregnancy was now far advanced, one day she said to Joseph: "My master, it is time that we prepare the things necessary for the birth of my holy Son. If you give me your permission, I will make the various clothes ready. I have already woven a piece of linen for His first swaddling clothes.

"Now please try to find some woolen cloth of soft texture and plain color for the other coverings. Later on I will weave a seamless tunic for Him. But let us pray to the Lord together for guidance in treating Him worthily."

Then as they knelt in prayer, each heard a Voice saying: "I have come from heaven to earth in order to exalt humility and discredit pride, to honor poverty and scorn riches, to destroy vanity and establish truth, and to enhance the value of labor. For this reason, it is My will that exteriorly you treat

Me according to the humble position that I have assumed, as if I were your natural child, and that interiorly you love and revere Me as the Man-God, Son of My Eternal Father."

Soon in exchange for his work Joseph obtained two pieces of woolen cloth of the best quality available, one white and the other gray. Of these Mary made the first little robes for her Son. From the linen which she had already woven as a present for the Temple, beginning the first day in her home in Nazareth, she made the swaddling clothes.

While doing this work for the Child in her womb, she remained on her knees all the time and often shed tears of devotion and love. From some flowers and herbs that Joseph gathered, she extracted fragrant essences and sprinkled them over the clothes. Then she folded them neatly and laid them away in a chest, saying to herself:

"My sweetest Love, when shall my eyes enjoy the light of Your divine face? When shall I as Your mother receive my Beloved's tender kiss? But how shall someone like me, so poor and insignificant, ever be able to treat You worthily? Look graciously upon me and let me take part in all the labors of Your life, since You are my Son and my Lord."

# CHAPTER FIVE

# THE JOURNEY TO BETHLEHEM

ONE day, Joseph, while away from home on an errand, heard that a recently proclaimed Roman edict ordered all heads of families in Palestine to be registered on the tax lists in their native cities. When he sadly told Mary this disturbing news, she answered reassuringly: "Do not let this edict cause you any concern, for all that happens to us is ordained by the Lord, and in all events His providence will assist and direct us."

"Nevertheless," said Joseph anxiously, "please pray that I may not have to be separated from you, for my heart would not have a moment's peace away from you, and I dare not leave you alone without help. But your delivery is too near for me to ask you to go with me to Bethlehem, for I fear to place you at any risk, because of your condition and my poverty. I would be heartbroken if the birth should occur on the way amid inconveniences that I could not alleviate."

Mary obediently presented Joseph's petitions to God, although she already knew that her divine Son was to be born in Bethlehem. And she received the following answer to her prayer: "My dearest dove, accompany My servant Joseph on the journey.

I shall be with you and I shall assist you with fatherly love in the tribulations you will suffer for My sake. Although they will be very great, do not fear."

Her heart being thus prepared for what lay ahead, Mary calmly told Joseph that she was going to travel with him. He was filled with joyful consolation, and thanking the Lord, he said to her: "My Lady, now my only source of grief will be the hardships you will have to undergo. But in Bethlehem we shall find friends and relatives, and there you will be able to rest from the journey."

Mary said nothing about the trying circumstances that she knew the Lord had decreed for His birth, though she fully realized that they would be far different from what Joseph expected. She always kept to herself all the secrets of God that she was not told to reveal. Instead, she now said to her good husband, quietly and humbly: "My master, I will accompany you with great joy. And we will make this journey as poor people, in the name of the Lord, for He will not despise poverty, which He has come to seek with so much love. Relying on His help, we will go with confidence to Bethlehem."

One night an angel appeared to him and said that he should set out at once with Mary for Bethlehem, as it was there that her Child was to be born. The angel told him, moreover, that he should provide himself with a few necessities. Then he noted all the items he was to take with them. Joseph was very much surprised.

The saint was also told that, besides the donkey on which Mary was to ride, he was to take with him a little female donkey, one year old, which had not yet given birth. This little animal they were to let run at large, and then follow the road it would take.

Anne was visiting Joseph and Mary in their house at Nazareth. Joseph told the two of them about the commands he had received, and they began to prepare for the journey. Anne was very much troubled about it. Though the Blessed Virgin had received an interior admonition that she would give birth to her child in Bethlehem, in her humility she had kept silence, so she had not revealed this to her mother.

Mary knew this, as well, from the prophecies in Scripture. She kept all the prophecies referring to the birth of the Messiah in her little closet at Nazareth; she read them often and prayed for their fulfillment. From those prophecies she knew that the Savior would be born in Bethlehem, so she lovingly submitted to the Divine Will and began her journey. It was a very painful one for her, since at that season it was cold in the mountains.

Joseph and Mary silently set out upon their journey with Anne; Mary's relative, Mary of Clopas [Jn 19:25]; and some servants. They started out from Anne's house. The donkey bore a comfortable saddle for Mary and her baggage.

In the same place where the angel had appeared to Joseph, Anne had a pasture ground. Here the servants went to fetch the little one-year-old female donkey that Joseph had to take with him. She ran after the Holy Family. Anne, Mary of Clopas, and the servants now parted from Joseph and Mary after a touching farewell.

The two travelers went some distance farther and lodged at a house that lay on very high ground. They were well received. The proprietor was the lease holder of the farm to which the field belonged. From it one could see far into the distance, even to the mountains near Jerusalem.

The next day, the Holy Family made their way through a very cold valley, toward a mountain. The ground was covered with frost and snow. They had travelled about four hours from where they had lodged, and Mary was suffering terribly from the cold.

She stopped near a pine tree and cried out: "We must rest! I can go no farther." Joseph arranged a seat for her under the tree, and placed a light in the tree.

The Blessed Virgin prayed fervently, imploring God not to allow them to freeze. At once so great a warmth passed into her that she stretched out her hands to Joseph so that he could warm himself by them. She took some food to renew her strength.

The little donkey, their guide, came with them here and then stood still. The actions of the little animal were truly astonishing. On straight roads, between mountains, for instance, where they could not go astray, she was sometimes behind, sometimes far ahead of them. But where the road branched, she was sure to make her appearance and run on the right way. Whenever they reached a spot at which they should stop, the little creature stood still.

Joseph here spoke to Mary of the good lodgings that he expected to find in Bethlehem. He told her that he knew the good people of an inn at which, for a moderate sum, they could get a comfortable room. It was better, he said, to pay a little than to depend upon free quarters. He praised the people of Bethlehem in order to console and encourage her.

After that, the Holy Family arrived at a large farmhouse about two hours' distance from the tree where they had stopped. It was about twelve hours from Nazareth. The woman was not at home, and the man refused Joseph admittance, telling him that he must go on farther. On they went until they came to a shepherd's shed, where they found the little donkey, and where they too stopped.

There were some shepherds in it, but they soon vacated after showing themselves most friendly and supplying straw and bundles of sticks for a fire. The shepherds then went to the house from which Mary and Joseph had been sent away. They mentioned having met them.

"What a beautiful, what an extraordinary woman!" they said. "What an amiable, pious, benevolent man! What wonderful people those travelers are!"

The man's wife had now returned home, and she scolded her husband for having sent Mary and Joseph away. She went to the shepherd's hut in which they had settled, but at first she was timid and dared not enter. Finally, she returned with her two children.

The woman was quite friendly and seemed to be deeply touched by what she saw. The husband also came and begged pardon. After Mary and Joseph had refreshed themselves a little, he showed them to an inn about an hour farther up the mountain.

The host there, however, gave the excuse to Joseph that there was no more room at the inn. But when the Blessed Virgin entered and begged for shelter, the wife of the innkeeper, as also the innkeeper himself, changed their attitude toward them. The man at once arranged a shelter for them under a neighboring shed and took charge of the donkey that Mary had been riding.

The little donkey was not with them. She was running around the fields. Whenever she was not needed, she did not make her appearance.

This inn was a tolerably fine one, and consisted of several houses. Although situated on the north side of the mountain, it was surrounded by orchards, pleasure gardens, and balsam trees. Mary and Joseph remained overnight and the whole of the next day, for it was the Sabbath.

On the Sabbath, the hostess with her three children visited Mary, along with the woman of that other house with her two children. Mary talked to the little ones and instructed them. They had little scrolls of parchment from which they read.

Joseph went out with the host to his fields. Both host and hostess had conceived great love for Mary; they sympathized with her condition. They pressed her to remain and showed her a room they would give her. But very early the next morning she started out with Joseph to continue their journey.

They went forward, a little more to the east, along the mountain and into a valley, increasing the distance between them and Samaria, to which they seemed at first to be going. The Samaritan temple upon Mount Gerizim was in sight. On the roof were numerous figures such as lions or other animals, which shone with a white light in the sun.

The road led down into a plain, to the field of Shechem. After a journey of several miles, they came to a solitary farmhouse where they were made welcome. The man was an overseer of fields and orchards belonging to a neighboring city.

It was warmer here, and vegetation was more luxuriant than at any place they had been, for it was the sunny side of the mountain. That made a great difference in Palestine at this season. The house was not exactly in the valley, but on the southern slope of the mountain that stretches from Samaria to the east.

The occupants were those shepherds whose daughters would later on marry the servants remaining behind from the caravan of the three kings. In later years, Jesus would often stay here and teach. Before departing, Joseph blessed the children of the family.

Next, Mary and Joseph journeyed over the plain beyond Shechem. The Blessed Virgin sometimes went on foot. They rested occasionally and refreshed themselves. They had with them little rolls and a cool, strengthening drink in nice little jugs, brown and shining like metal.

The saddle that Mary used on the donkey was furnished with a pad on either side as a support for the limbs, which were brought by it into more of a sitting posture. The support was over the neck of the donkey, and Mary sat sometimes to the right, sometimes to the left. Berries and other fruits were still hanging on the bushes and trees that were exposed to the sun, and these they gathered on the way.

The first thing that Joseph always did on arriving at an inn was to prepare a comfortable bed for Mary. Then he washed his feet, and Mary did as well. Their washings were frequent.

It was quite dark one evening when they reached a lonely inn. Joseph knocked and begged for shelter, but the owner would not open the door. Joseph explained to him his position, telling him that his wife could go no farther. But the man was inflexible; he would not interrupt his own rest.

When Joseph told him that he would pay him, he received this reply: "This is not an inn. I will not have that knocking." The door remained closed.

Mary and Joseph went on for a short distance and found a shed. He struck a light and prepared a resting place for Mary, as she assisted him. He brought the donkey in and found some straw and fodder for it.

Here they rested a few hours. Early the next morning they departed while it was still dark. They were now about six hours distant from their previous stopping place, about twenty-six from Nazareth, and ten from Jerusalem. The last house stood on level ground, but the road to Jerusalem began again to grow steep.

Up to this time, Mary and Joseph chose to avoid great highways as they traveled, though they crossed several commercial routes that ran from the Jordan to Samaria and to the roads that lead from Syria down into Egypt. So far, the roads by which they came, with the exception of that single broad one, were very narrow and ran over the mountains. They had to be very cautious in walking, but the donkey could tread its way securely.

The travelers next arrived at a house whose owner was at first uncivil to Joseph. He threw the light on Mary's face, and made fun of Joseph for having so young a wife. But the man's wife took them in, gave them shelter in an out building, and offered them some little rolls.

When they left this place, they next sought lodging in a large farmhouse where once again they were not received in a cordial manner. The innkeepers were young and paid little heed to Mary and Joseph. They were not simple shepherds, but rich farmers, mixed up with the world, with trade, and so on.

Not all the lodgings the Holy Family encountered on the way to Bethlehem were so unfriendly. At one inn where they stopped, the innkeeper was a very round peasant woman who received Mary and Joseph with great gladness and made constant efforts to entertain them. When Mary entered the inn, the hostess came in, gave Mary a gentle touch, and invited her to warm herself by the fireplace in a grand room nearby where distinguished guests would sit. But the Virgin, thanking her very much for the favor she was offered, did not accept the gift, excusing herself with graciousness and humility.

Instead, Mary took her place by a fire where there was gathered a crowd of guests who were obviously poor. They were all dining at various small tables. The tableware was the kind used in poor homes, made of rough wood.

The good woman walked anxiously beside the Virgin and told those who were dining: "A Lady has come, beautiful, modest, and discreet; and as much as I desire to know who she is, yet I cannot say. But without a doubt she must be some great person, quite prominent." And they all wanted to know who Mary was.

Next the pious hostess went to fetch a very rough earthenware bowl, filled it with broth, placed it on an earthenware plate, and brought it to Mary with other food, which she had chosen from the best dishes she had served the other guests. The Lady received it from the hand of the devout peasant woman with joy and great gratitude. Then Joseph began his meal with a very white, ring-shaped bread roll.

That evening, once Joseph and Mary had retired, angels came down from heaven to fill the inn with their melodies. They sang the sweetest of tunes, accompanied by the soft music of the instruments they played, creating a celestial harmony.

The next day, the devout innkeeper, with great pleasure, escorted them outside as they prepared to set out again for Bethlehem. Placing her hand on the good woman's shoulder, Mary said to her: "May the Lord Almighty repay you, sister, for the fine hospitality you have shown." Then Mary and Joseph continued their journey.

They still had seven hours to travel. But they did not take the direct route there, because it was mountainous and at this season too difficult. Instead, they followed the little donkey across the country between Jerusalem and the Jordan.

The Holy Family arrived about noon at the large house of a shepherd, about two hours from what would one day be John's place of baptizing in the Jordan. Many years later, Jesus would once pass a night there after His baptism. Near the house was another building for the farm and sheep utensils, and in the yard was a spring from which the water was conducted through pipes to the bathtubs.

There was a large inn here, and a number of servants who took their meals there were going and coming. The host received the travelers very kindly, and he was very obliging. He insisted upon one of the servant's washing Joseph's feet at the spring. He also supplied Joseph with fresh garments while he aired and then brushed those he took off. A maidservant rendered the same services to Mary.

At their departure, about noon, Mary and Joseph were accompanied part of the way by some of the people belonging to the inn. They traveled westward toward Bethlehem. After a journey of about two hours, they arrived at a little village consisting of a long row of houses with gardens and courts lying on both sides of a broad high road.

Joseph had connections here, such as the kind that might arise from the second marriage of a stepfather or stepmother. Their house was finely situated and very handsome. But Mary and Joseph did not enter.

Instead, they passed through the place and went straight on toward Jerusalem for half an hour, when they came to an inn where a crowd was gathered for a funeral. The proprietors of the house, who were preoccupied with being in charge of the funeral, left to the servants the duty of receiving Mary and Joseph. This was done accordingly, and the customary services were rendered to the holy travelers. After some time, the people of the house engaged in conversation with Mary and Joseph.

Early the following morning, Mary and Joseph again started off. The good wife of the house told them they might stay, because Mary appeared to be ready to deliver her baby at any time. But Mary said with lowered veil that she still had thirty-six or thirty-eight hours. The woman was anxious to keep them, though not in her own house.

As Joseph and Mary were departing, the husband talked with Joseph about his beasts. Joseph praised the donkey highly and told him that he had brought the other with him in case of necessity. When their hosts spoke of the difficulty of getting lodgings in Bethlehem, Joseph replied that he had friends there and that Mary and he would certainly be well received.

Joseph always spoke this way of his expectations for lodging in Bethlehem with great confidence. He made the same remark to Mary on their way. But he would soon be disappointed.

On the last days of the journey, when they were nearing Bethlehem, Mary sighed longingly for rest and refreshment. Joseph turned aside from the road for half an hour to a place where, on a former occasion, he had discovered a beautiful fig tree laden with fruit. It had seats around it where weary wayfarers could rest.

When they reached the tree they found, to their great disappointment, that it was at that time quite barren of fruit. In fact, it would never again bear fruit, though it remained green. In later years, Jesus would search that same fig tree for fruit. He would find it still barren and curse it, and it would wither [Mt 21:18–22].

The distance from the last inn to Bethlehem was about three hours. Mary and Joseph went around by the north and approached the city on the west. The weather was lovely, not at all cold, with the sun lighting up the mountain between Jerusalem and Bethany.

A short distance outside the city, about a quarter of an hour's walk brought them to a large building surrounded by courtyards and smaller houses. There were trees in front of it, and all sorts of people encamped in tents around it. This house was once Joseph's father's house, and ages before it had been the family mansion of David. It was at this period used as the custom house for the Roman taxes.

The little donkey was not with them here. She had run away around the south side of the city, where it was somewhat level, a kind of valley.

Joseph still had in the city a stepbrother, who was an innkeeper. Joseph did not go near him. Instead, he went straight into the custom house, for all newcomers had to present themselves there and obtain a ticket for entrance to the city. The city had properly no gate, but the entrance lay between two ruined walls that looked like the remains of a gate. Although Joseph was somewhat late in presenting himself for assessment, he was well received.

Mary remained in a small house in the courtyard among the women. They were very attentive to her and offered her something to eat. These women cooked for the soldiers, who were Romans.

There were a number of clerks and functionaries in the customs house, scattered throughout the different rooms. A great many Romans and soldiers were found in the upper stories. There were also Pharisees and Sadducees, priests and elders, and all sorts of clerks and officials, both Jewish and Roman. The writing and the movement back and forth were incessant.

Joseph went up to a large room in an upper story, where he was interrogated about who he was and other matters. His questioners examined long written scrolls, many of which were hanging on the walls. They unrolled them and read to him his ancestry, as well as Mary's. Joseph had not known before then that through Mary's father, Joachim, she was descended in a straight line from David.

For seven years the inhabitants of this part of the country had not been regularly assessed, owing to various political troubles. The current tax collecting had already been going on for many months, but two payments were still to be made. They had in fact paid something here and there during those seven years, but there had been no regular collection of taxes.

Joseph did not pay anything on that first day, but he was queried about his circumstances. He told the official that he possessed no real estate, that he lived by his trade and the assistance of his wife's mother. So the official asked him, "Where is your wife?"

Then Mary was also summoned to appear before the clerk, but not upstairs. She was interrogated in a passage on the first floor, and nothing was read to her. Finally, Joseph was allowed to take Mary straight to Bethlehem (on whose outskirts the houses stood scattered) and into the heart of the city.

# CHAPTER SIX

# *THE NATIVITY*

AT the different street intersections they encountered in Bethlehem, Joseph left Mary and the donkey standing while he went up and down in search of an inn. Mary often had to wait long before Joseph, anxious and troubled, returned.

Nowhere did he find room. Everywhere he was sent away. And now it began to grow dark.

Joseph at last proposed going to the other side of the city, where they would surely find lodgings. They proceeded down a street, which was more of a country road than a city street, for the houses stood scattered along the hills. At the end of it they reached a low, level field.

Here stood a very beautiful tree with a smooth trunk, its branches spreading out like a roof. Joseph led Mary and the beast under it, and left them there to go again in search of an inn. As long as she remained under it, the tree was quite green and afforded ample shelter. But when she left it, it resumed its wintry nakedness. This was perhaps only a sign of reverence, but the Blessed Virgin was fully conscious of it.

Joseph went from house to house, but his friends, of whom he had spoken to Mary, were unwilling to recognize him. Once during his search, he returned to Mary, waiting under the tree. He wept, and she consoled him. Then he started afresh on his quest. But whenever he mentioned the approaching delivery of his wife as a pressing reason for receiving hospitality, he was dismissed still more quickly.

Meantime, it had grown fully dark. Mary was standing under the tree, her ungirdled robe falling around her in full folds, her head covered with a white veil. The donkey was nearby, its head turned toward the tree, at the foot of which Joseph had made a seat for Mary with the baggage.

Crowds were hurrying back and forth in Bethlehem, and many of the passersby gazed curiously at Mary, as one naturally does on seeing a person standing a long time in the dark. Some of them addressed her, and asked her who she was. Little did they dream that the Savior was so near!

Mary was so patient, so tranquil, so full of hope. She had so long to wait. At last she sat down, with her hands crossed on her breast and her head lowered.

After a long time, Joseph returned in great dejection. He was shedding tears. Because he had failed again to find an inn, he hesitated to approach.

But suddenly he recalled a cave outside Bethlehem used as a storage place by the shepherds when they brought their cattle to the city. As a youth, Joseph had often withdrawn there to conceal himself from his brothers and to pray. It was very likely to be deserted at that season or, if any shepherds did come, it would be easy to make friends with them. He and Mary might find there shelter for a while, and after a little rest he would go out again on his search.

Now they left the tree and wound their way toward a hill and climbed it. Then the road began again to descend. At last, they reached another hill before which stood trees—firs, pines, or cedars—and trees with small leaves like the box tree.

In this hill was the cave spoken of by Joseph. There were no houses around. One side of the cave was built up with rough masonry through which the open entrance of the shepherds led down into the valley.

The cave lay at the end of the mountain ridge of Bethlehem. A clump of beautiful trees stood in front of the entrance. From there could be viewed some of the towers and roofs of the city.

Joseph opened the light wicker door and, as they entered, the little donkey ran to meet them. She had left them near Joseph's old home and had run around the city to this cave. She frolicked around and leapt gaily about them, so that Mary said: "Look! It is surely God's will that we should be here." But Joseph was worried and, in secret, a little ashamed, because he had so often alluded to the good reception they would meet in Bethlehem.

There was a ledge of rock above the door; he stood the donkey under it. Then Joseph arranged a place for Mary to sit. It was quite dark, about eight o'clock, when they reached this place. Joseph struck a light and went into the cave.

The entrance was very narrow. The walls were stuffed with all kinds of coarse straw, overlaid with brown mats. Back in the vaulted part were some airholes in the roof, but there also everything was in disorder.

Joseph cleared it out and prepared enough space in the back part to allow reclining room for Mary, who had seated herself on a rug with her bundle for a support. The donkey was then brought in. Joseph fastened a lamp on the wall.

While Mary was eating, he went out to the field and laid a leather bottle in the stream to fill it. He went also to the city, where he procured some little dishes of food, a bundle of other items, and some fruit. It was, in fact, the Sabbath, but on account of the numerous strangers in the city and their need for various necessaries, provisions and utensils were set out for sale on tables placed at the street corners. Servants or pagan slaves guarded the tables, and the price was paid on the spot.

When Joseph returned, he brought with him a small bundle of slender sticks beautifully bound up with reeds, and a box with a handle in which were glowing coals. These he poured out at the entrance of the cave to make a fire. He next brought the water bottle that he had filled at the stream, then prepared some food. It consisted of a stew made of grain and vegetables, with a little bread.

After they had eaten, Mary lay down to rest on her bed made of rushes, covered with a spread. Then Joseph began to prepare his own resting place at the entrance of the cave. Behind this cave was a small side cave just large enough to allow the donkey to stand upright. There the fodder was stored. A gutter ran along by this corner, and Joseph was cleaning out the cave. When this was done, he went again into the city.

Before setting out, he had stopped up all the openings of the cave, in order to keep out the night air. The Blessed Virgin knelt in prayer, then lay down upon the carpet on her side, with her head resting on her arm and her bundle serving for a pillow.

Beside the cave where Jesus was to be born, in the same hill but lying somewhat deeper, there were two other caves. In one of them, the Blessed Virgin could be secluded.

On the following day, Joseph prepared a place for Mary to sit and to lie down in yet another cave. It was more spacious than the first cave where the Child's crib would be located. Mary remained there some hours while Joseph was making the place more habitable. He also brought from the city many different little vessels and some dried fruits.

Mary told Joseph that the Child would be born the following night. It was then nine months since her conception by the Holy Spirit. She begged Joseph to do all in his power to make sure they would receive as honorably as possible this Child promised by God, this Child supernaturally conceived. And she invited him to unite with her in prayer for those hard-hearted people who would provide Him no shelter.

Joseph proposed to bring some pious women whom he knew in Bethlehem to her assistance. But Mary would not allow it. She declared that she had no need of anyone.

It was five o'clock in the evening when Joseph brought Mary back again to the crib cave. He hung up several more lamps and made a place under the shed in front of the door for the little donkey, which came joyfully hurrying from the fields to meet them.

When Mary told Joseph that her time was drawing near and that he should now withdraw to pray, he left her and turned toward his sleeping place to do as she asked. Before entering his little recess, he looked back once toward that part of the cave where Mary knelt upon her bed in prayer, with her back to him and her face toward the east. He saw the cave filled with the light that streamed from Mary, for she was entirely enveloped as if by flames.

It was as if he were, like Moses, looking into the burning bush. He sank prostrate to the ground in prayer and did not look back again. The glory around Mary became brighter and brighter, until the lamps that Joseph had lit were no longer to be seen.

Mary knelt, with her flowing white robe spread out before her. At midnight, her prayer became ecstatic, and she was raised so far above the ground that it was visible beneath her. Her hands were crossed upon her breast, and the light around her grew even more resplendent.

The roof of the cave was no longer visible. Instead, above Mary stretched a pathway of light up to heaven. In that path, it seemed as if one light came forth from another, as if one figure dissolved into another, and from these different spheres of light other heavenly figures issued.

Mary continued in prayer, with her eyes bent low toward the ground. At that moment she gave birth to the Infant Jesus. He appeared as a tiny, shining Child, lying on the rug at her knees, and brighter far than all the other brilliance. Even inanimate nature seemed stirred. The stones of the rocky floor and the walls of the cave were glimmering and sparkling, as if filled with life.

Mary's ecstasy lasted some moments longer. Then she spread a cover over the Child, but she did not yet hold Him or even touch Him. After a long time, the Child began to stir and cry, and only then did Mary seem to recover full consciousness.

She lifted the Child to her breast, both of them wrapped in a veil, and nursed Him. Angels were around her in human form lying prostrate on their faces.

About an hour after the birth, Mary called Joseph, who still lay prostrate in prayer. When he approached, he fell on his knees, his face to the ground, in a transport of joy, devotion, and humility. Then Mary said to him: "My husband and my helper, receive in your arms the Creator of heaven and earth, and enjoy His amiable and sweet company, so that my Lord and my God may be delighted and rewarded by your faithful services. Take to yourself the Treasure of the eternal Father and take part in this blessing of the human race."

Then, speaking interiorly to the divine Infant, she said: "Sweetest Love of my soul and Light of my eyes, rest in the arms of Joseph, my friend and spouse; hold sweet conversation with him and pardon me my shortcomings. I feel the loss of You deeply even for an instant, but I want to convey without envy the good I have received to all who are worthy."

Her most faithful husband, acknowledging this new blessing, humbled himself to the earth and answered: "Lady and sovereign of the world, my spouse, how can I, being so unworthy, presume to hold in my arms God Himself, in whose presence tremble the pillars of heaven? How can I have courage to accept such an exalted favor? I am but dust and ashes, but assist me, Lady, in my lowliness, and ask His Majesty to look upon me with mercy and make me worthy through His grace."

His desire to hold the infant God, and his reverential fear of Him, caused within Joseph heroic acts of love, faith, humility, and the most profound reverence. Trembling with prudent fear, he received Jesus from the hands of His most holy mother, while sweetest tears of joy and delight abundantly flowed from his eyes with an extraordinary happiness. The divine Infant looked at Joseph lovingly and at the same time renewed the saint's inmost soul with such divine power that no words could explain.

Joseph broke out in new canticles of praise at seeing himself enriched with such magnificent blessings and favors. After having for some time enjoyed in spirit the sweetest effects of holding in his arms the Lord, who encompasses heaven and earth, he returned Him to the arms of His fortunate mother, as both of them knelt to give and receive Him. His most prudent mother observed a similar reverence every time she took Him up or gave Him to Joseph, and Joseph imitated her reverence as often as it was his happy lot to hold the incarnate Word. Whenever they approached His Majesty, they also made three genuflections, kissing the earth and making heroic acts of humility, worship, and reverence. In this way both the great Queen and the blessed Joseph expressed the proper reverence in receiving or giving the Child one to the other.

Mary wrapped the Babe in red and white and laid Him in the crib, which had been filled with rushes and fine moss, over which was spread a cover that hung down at the sides. The crib stood over a stone trough, and at this spot the ground stretched straight and level. The floor of this part of the cave lay somewhat deeper than where the Child was born, and down to it steps had been formed in the earth. When Mary laid the Child in the crib, both she and Joseph stood by Him in tears, singing the praises of God.

The seat and the bed prepared by Joseph for the Blessed Virgin were near the crib. On the first day after the birth, she sat upright or rested on her side, with no indicators of weakness or sickness. Both before and after the birth, she was robed in white.

# CHAPTER SEVEN

## *THE SHEPHERDS' VISIT AND THE CIRCUMCISION OF JESUS*

O N the night of the birth there gushed forth a beautiful spring in the other cave that lay beside it. The water spilled out, and the next day Joseph dug a course for it and formed a spring.

On that night was extraordinary gladness in many places, even in the most distant regions of the world, with things to be marveled at. As a result, the good were filled with joyful longings, and the bad with dread. Many of the lower animals were joyfully stirred up. Fountains were gushing forth and swelling, flowers springing up in many places, trees and plants budding with new life, and all sending forth their fragrance.

In Bethlehem, it was misty. The sky above shone with a murky, reddish glare. But over the valley of the shepherds, around the crib cave and in the valley, floated bright clouds of refreshing dew.

The herds of the three oldest shepherds stood near the hill under sheds. But those further on, near the shepherds' tower, were partly in the open air. The three eldest shepherds, roused by the wonders of the night, stood together before their huts, gazing around and pointing out a magnificent light that shone over the crib.

The shepherds at the distant tower were also fully engaged. They had climbed up the tower and were looking toward the crib cave, over which they, too, saw the light.

A cloud of glory descended upon the three shepherds. In it figures were moving back and forth, and sweet, clear voices were singing softly. At first, the shepherds were frightened. Soon there stood before them seven lovely, radiant figures holding in their hands a long strip like a scroll on which were written words in letters half a foot in length. The angels were singing the *Gloria* [see Lk 2:14].

These angels appeared also to the shepherds on the tower. But the men did not hurry off at once to the cave. The first three were in fact an hour and a half distant from it, and those on the tower twice as far. But they began at once to reflect upon what gifts they should take to the newborn Savior, and to get them together as quickly as possible. Then the three shepherds went to the crib cave early the next morning.

Anne at Nazareth, Elizabeth in her village, Noemi (Mary's former governess), Anna and Simeon in the Temple—all had on this night visions from which they learned about the birth of the Savior. The child John was unspeakably joyful. But only Anne knew where the newborn Child was. The others, and even Elizabeth, knew of Mary and saw her in a vision. But they knew nothing of Bethlehem.

Then something terrifying took place in the Temple in Jerusalem. The writings of the Sadducees were more than once hurled by an invisible force from the places in which they were kept, which caused these men inexplicable dread. The event was ascribed to sorcery, and large sums of money were paid to hush the matter up.

Meanwhile, a series of great wonders appeared in the heavens in the country of the three magi, who had been observing the skies carefully. A star shot suddenly from its place and skimmed along the heavens before them. It was for them a sign announcing as never before that the Child, so long awaited by them and by their ancestors, was at last born in Judea, and that they were to follow that star.

For some nights immediately preceding that blessed one, they had from their observation tower seen all kinds of visions in the heavens, with kings journeying to the Child and offering their homage to Him. So now they hurriedly gathered together their treasures, and with gifts and presents they began the journey, for they did not want to be the last to arrive.

In the early dawn after the birth of Jesus, the three oldest of the shepherds came to the crib cave with the gifts they had gathered together. These consisted of little animals bearing some resemblance to deer. They were very lightly built and nimble, and they had long necks and clear, beautiful eyes. They followed or ran alongside the shepherds who led them with thin, guiding cords. The shepherds also carried large, live birds under their arms, and dead ones for food slung over their shoulders.

They told Joseph at the entrance of the cave what the angel had announced to them, and that they had come to do homage to the Child of promise and to offer Him gifts. Joseph accepted their presents and allowed them to lead the animals into the space that formed a kind of cellar near the side entrance of the cave. Then he led them to the Blessed Virgin, who was sitting on the ground near the crib, with a rug under her and the Infant Jesus on her lap.

The shepherds, with their staffs resting on their arms, fell on their knees and wept with joy. They knelt a long while, tasting great interior sweetness, then intoned the canticle of praise they had heard from the angels, along with a psalm. When they were about to take leave, Mary placed the Child in their arms.

Some of the other shepherds came in the evening, accompanied by women and children, and bringing gifts. They sang most sweetly before the crib the *Gloria*, some Psalms, and short refrains with these words: "O Child, You are blooming as a rose! As a herald You come forth!" They brought gifts of birds, eggs, honey, woven fabrics of various colors, bundles of raw silk, and grain.

The three oldest shepherds came back in turn and helped Joseph to make the crib cave and its surroundings more comfortable. Several pious women were with the Blessed Virgin, performing some services for her. They belonged to the Jewish sect known as the Essenes, and they lived in the valley, not far from the crib cave, in little rocky cells adjoining one another. They owned little gardens near their cells, and they taught the children of their community.

Joseph had invited them to come, for he had been acquainted with them even in his early youth. When he had hidden from his brothers in the crib cave, he had visited these pious women who dwelt in the side of the rock. They now came in turn to the Blessed Virgin, bringing little necessities and bundles of wood. They cooked and washed for the Holy Family.

Some days after the birth of Jesus, there was an especially touching scene in the crib cave. Joseph and Mary were standing by the crib and gazing with deep feeling upon the Infant Jesus, when suddenly the donkey fell on her knees and lowered her head to the ground. Mary and Joseph shed tears at the sight.

While Mary was still standing by the crib in deep meditation, some shepherds drew near with their wives, five persons in all. To give them room to approach the crib, the Blessed Virgin withdrew a little to the spot where she had given birth to the Child. The people did not actually adore Him, but they gazed down upon the Child deeply moved, and before leaving, they bowed low over Him as if kissing Him.

It was daytime. Mary sat in her usual place with the Infant Jesus on her lap. He was swaddled, the hands and face alone free. Mary had something like a piece of linen in her hands with which she was busied.

Joseph was at the fireplace near the entrance of the cave. He appeared to be making a shelf to hold some vessels. Then in came three aged female Essenes, who were cordially welcomed, though Mary did not rise.

They brought quite a number of gifts: small fruits; birds with red, awl-shaped beaks as large as ducks, which they carried by the wings; oval rolls about an inch in thickness; some linen; and other items. All were received with rare humility and gratitude. The women were very silent and recollected. Deeply moved, they gazed down upon the Child, but they did not touch Him. When they withdrew, it was without farewells or ceremony.

Now came two married women with three little girls about eight years old. They appeared to be strangers and people of distinction, who had come in obedience to a call more miraculous than that received by any previous visitor. Joseph welcomed them very humbly and behaved with great humility during such visits, withdrawing and looking on from some distant corner.

They brought gifts smaller in size than the others, but of greater value: grain in a bowl, small fruits, and a cluster of thick, triangular, golden leaves on which was a stamp like a seal. Mary rose and placed the Child in the ladies' arms. Both held Him a little while, praying silently with uplifted heart, and then kissed Him. The three little girls were silent and deeply impressed. Joseph and Mary then spoke with their visitors, and when they left, Joseph accompanied them part of the way.

The day after, the Blessed Virgin and the Infant Jesus left the crib cave with the maid for some hours. Stepping from the door of the cave, Mary turned toward the shed on the right, went some steps forward, and concealed herself in that side cave where, at the birth of Jesus, a spring had welled up.

She remained there four hours, because some men, spies of Herod, had come from Bethlehem, provoked by the rumor set afloat by the words of the shepherds that a miracle had taken place there in connection with a child. These men met Joseph in front of the crib cave. After exchanging a few words with him, they left him with contemptuous smiles at his humility and simplicity.

The crib cave was secluded and very pleasantly situated. No one from Bethlehem went there, only the shepherds whose duties called them there. No one in Bethlehem took any interest in what was going on beyond the town, because the influx of strangers made the city all alive, and much buying and selling was going on. Cattle were being bought and slaughtered, for many people paid their taxes in cattle. There were numerous pagans in the city who were serving as servants.

Reports about the marvel of the angels' appearance was soon spread among the dwellers of the mountain valleys far and near, and with it the birth of the Child in the cave. The various innkeepers from whom the Holy Family on their journey had received hospitality now came, one after another, to do homage to Him whom they had unknowingly entertained. The hospitable keeper of the last inn first sent gifts by a servant, then came himself to honor the Child.

The good wife of that man who had been so cross to Joseph visited as well, along with other shepherds and good people. They were deeply moved by what they saw. All were in holiday attire and were going up to Bethlehem for the Sabbath. The good wife could have gone to Jerusalem, which was nearer, but she preferred coming to Bethlehem.

One of Joseph's relatives also came to the crib cave on his way to Bethlehem for the Sabbath. He was the father of the man named Jonadab who, many years later, at the crucifixion of Jesus, would present a strip of linen to Him. Joseph was very kind to him.

This relative had heard from people of his neighborhood about Joseph's amazing situation, so he came to bring him gifts and to visit the Infant Jesus and Mary. But Joseph would not accept anything. He did, however, pawn the little donkey to this relative with the understanding that she might be later redeemed for the same amount of money received.

After that, Mary, Joseph, the maid, and two of the shepherds who were standing in front of the entrance celebrated the Sabbath in the crib cave. A lamp with seven wicks was lighted. On a small table covered with white and red lay the prayer scrolls.

The numerous foods presented by the shepherds were either given to the poor or handed around for the enjoyment of others. The birds prepared for cooking were hung on a spit before the fire, turned from time to time, and sprinkled with the flour of a reed-like plant that was quite plentiful around the area of

Bethlehem and Hebron. From its grain a shining, white jelly was prepared and cakes were baked. Under the fireplace were hot, clean holes in which other birds could be roasted.

After the Sabbath, the Essene women prepared a meal out under the arbor which Joseph, with the help of the shepherds, had put up at the entrance of the cave. Joseph went into the city to engage priests for the circumcision of the Child. The cave was cleared and put in order. The partition that Joseph had put up in the passage was removed, and the ground was spread with carpets, for in this passage near the crib cave they prepared a place for the ceremony.

Mary and Joseph had previously discussed which name was to be given to the divine Infant in the circumcision. Joseph said: "My Lady, when the holy angel of the Most High informed me of this great mystery, he also told me that your most sacred Son should be called *Jesus*."

The Virgin Mother answered: "This same name was revealed to me when He assumed flesh in my womb. Since we have received this name from the Most High through the mouth of His holy angels, His ministers, it is fitting that we act in humble reverence according to the hidden and mysterious judgments of His infinite wisdom in conferring it on my Son and Lord. We will call Him *Jesus*. This name we will give the priest to be inscribed in the register of the other circumcised children."

Joseph returned from Bethlehem with five priests and a woman whose services were necessary on such occasions. They brought with them the circumcision stool and an octangular stone with all that was needed for the ceremony. All this was arranged in the cave passage.

That evening a meal was spread under the arbor at the entrance to the cave. A crowd of poor people had followed the priests, as is usual on such occasions. During the meal they continually received gifts both from the priests and from Joseph.

The priests went to Mary and the Child, spoke with the mother, and took the Child in their arms. They also spoke to Joseph about the name the Child was to receive. They prayed and sang the greater part of the night, then circumcised the

Child at daybreak. Mary was quite troubled and concerned about Him.

After the ceremony, the Infant Jesus was swaddled in red and white, and His head was wrapped in a cloth. The Child was again laid on the octangular stone, which had been placed at the spot where He was born. Then prayers were recited over Him.

One of the priests did not at first approve of the name Jesus, so they continued to pray. Then a radiant angel stood in front of the priest and held before him a tablet like the one nailed to the top of the Cross. On it was inscribed the name *Jesus.*

Deeply moved, on a scrap of parchment he wrote the name *Jesus* under divine inspiration. After that, Joseph received the Child back. He handed Him to the Blessed Virgin who, with two other women, was standing back in the crib cave. Mary took the weeping Child into her arms and quieted Him.

Some shepherds were standing at the entrance of the cave. Lamps were burning, and the dawn was breaking. There was some more praying and singing, then before the priests departed, they took a little breakfast.

All present at the circumcision were good people. The priests were enlightened and later attained salvation. Alms were distributed the whole morning to many poor people who presented themselves.

During the day, the nurse was again with Mary attending to Jesus. That night, the Child was very restless from pain. He cried, and Mary and Joseph tried to soothe Him by carrying Him up and down the passage of the cave.

In the Temple at Jerusalem, Hanukkah, the holy Feast of the Maccabees, began at this time. It was also celebrated by Joseph in the crib cave. He fastened three lamps with seven little lights on the walls of the cave and, throughout a whole week, lit them morning and evening.

Once during this time, there came to the cave one of the priests who had been present at the Child's circumcision. He had a scroll of writings with prayers that he prayed with Joseph. Apparently, he wanted to find out whether Joseph kept that feast or not.

Mary later told Joseph how she had seen in spirit that great kings from the East, the magi, were approaching with rich gifts, and that their coming would attract much attention. To prepare everything for their arrival, Joseph set to work to clear out the crib cave as well as those caves beside it. He also went to Bethlehem to make the second payment of taxes and to look around for a permanent home, because he intended to settle in Bethlehem after Mary's purification.

# ❧ CHAPTER EIGHT ❧

## THE VISIT OF THE MAGI

AMONG some pious people in Judea was an expectation of the soon coming of the Messiah, and the circumstances surrounding the birth of Jesus had been spread abroad by the shepherds. Herod had heard all that and had at Bethlehem made secret inquiries into the situation. His spies, however, having found only poor Joseph, and also having orders not to attract attention, reported that it was nothing, that they had found only a poor family from Nazareth living in a cave, and that the whole affair was not worth talking about.

But now, all of a sudden, there appeared at Jerusalem a great caravan of the three kings, the magi. Their asking for the King of Judah was marked by such confidence and precision, and they spoke with such certainty about the star, that Herod could scarcely hide his anxious perplexity. He hoped to learn the particulars of the affair from the kings themselves, then take measures accordingly.

When sometime later the kings, warned by God, did not return, he attributed their departure to falsehood and disappointment. They were, he thought, ashamed to come back and be looked on as fools. So he issued a proclamation in Bethlehem and beyond that the people should have nothing to do with the strangers.

As we shall see, however, eventually the king sought to seize the infant Jesus, so he had his men search Nazareth. But he found that the Child was no longer there. Consequently, he commanded that a more extensive search be made for Him. When Herod had to give up all hope of finding Him and his anxiety was, as a result, considerably deepened, he made the desperate resolution to murder all the children in Bethlehem. He was so cautious in executing his measures that he sent his troops beforehand, in order to avoid any insurrection.

The kings left Jerusalem followed by a crowd as far as a brook outside the city. There, the rabble left them and turned back home. On the opposite side of the brook, the kings stopped and looked for their star. To their great joy, they saw it, and on again they went, singing sweetly. But the star did not guide them by a direct route from Jerusalem to Bethlehem. Instead, they went more to the west.

The star, which by night looked like a globe of light, now had the appearance of the moon when seen by day. But it did not appear exactly round; it was somewhat pointed. It was often hidden behind the clouds.

The highroad between Bethlehem and Jerusalem swarmed with people, travelers with their baggage on donkeys. They were, perhaps on account of the census, returning from Bethlehem to distant homes, or going up to Jerusalem to the Temple or the markets. But on the route taken by the kings, it was very quiet. The star guided them that way so that they might escape notice and arrive in Bethlehem in the evening.

It was twilight when the caravan drew up before Bethlehem at the same gate where Mary and Joseph had stopped. The star had disappeared. The kings went to the custom house, the former home of Joseph's parents, where Joseph and Mary had recently been enrolled.

Crowds of people thronged around the newcomers. The kings and their retinue dismounted and refreshed themselves. Here, they had thought, they would find the newborn King. When it became clear that He was not there, they still remained for some time, wrestling with doubt and anxiety about what to do next.

At last, a light rose in the heavens on the opposite side of Bethlehem over the region of the crib cave. The light was like that of the rising moon. The caravan again set out in that direction and passed the field in which Christ's birth had been announced to the shepherds.

Someone in Bethlehem had recommended that the kings choose the valley of the shepherds as a good place for setting up camp. A few of the locals followed the cavalcade as they went there, but the kings said nothing to them about the object of their search. The caravan filed down into the valley of the crib cave, dismounted, and began to set up their tents. Meanwhile, the people who had crowded after them from Bethlehem returned to the city.

The encampment was partly pitched when over the cave shone out the star once more, and in it a Child was plainly visible. It stood directly above the crib, its stream of light falling straight down on it. The kings and their followers uncovered their heads and watched it sinking lower and lower, increasing in size as it approached the earth. It looked as large as a sheet. All were at first amazed. It was already dark; no dwelling could be seen, only the hill of the crib cave, looking like a rampart on the plain.

Soon their amazement turned to joy, and they found the entrance of the cave. One king pushed back the door and there, in the upper end of the cave—resplendent with light—he saw Mary sitting with the Child, and looking just like the Virgin they had so often seen in their star visions. He stepped back and told his companions what he had seen.

Joseph had known they would be arriving that night, either because someone from Jerusalem had told him or because he saw it in a vision. So during the day he had been bringing all kinds of food from Bethlehem: fruit, honey, and vegetables. He had also cleared out the cave, making more room, taking away the partitions that cut off his own little sleeping place from the passage, and stowing away the wood and the cooking utensils under the shed in front of the door.

Joseph came out to them from the cave with an old shepherd, speaking to them in quite a friendly way. The kings told him in a few words that they had come to adore the newborn King of the Jews whose star they had seen, and to bring Him gifts. Joseph humbly welcomed them.

Both the ceremony and the gifts themselves were quite lavish. But the words of the kings and their followers were extraordinarily simple and childlike, as if they were inebriated with love. They always began: "We have seen His star and that He is King over all kings. We have come to adore Him and to bring Him gifts."

With the most tender tears and most fervent prayers, they commended to the Child Jesus themselves, their goods, and their property, all that they valued on earth. They begged Him to take their hearts, their souls, their actions, their thoughts. They entreated Him to enlighten them, to bestow upon them all the virtues, and to the whole earth to grant peace, happiness, and love.

They were glowing with love. No words could depict their fervor and humility, nor the tears of joy that bathed their cheeks and flowed down the beard of the eldest. They were perfectly happy; they believed that, at last, they had entered into the star after which their forefathers had so long legitimately sighed, and at which they themselves had so longingly gazed. All the joy of the promise of many hundreds of years now fulfilled welled up in their hearts.

Joseph and Mary also wept. The kings' honor paid their Child and Savior; the kings' recognition of that Child for whom their poverty could afford so poor a bed; the kings' knowledge of His high dignity that lay hidden in the silent humility of their own hearts—all this comforted them immeasurably.

Mary and Joseph saw brought to Him from so great a distance by God's almighty power, and in spite of the machinations of man, what they themselves could not procure for Him: the adoration of the great, and magnificent gifts offered with holy profusion. They adored alongside those great ones, and the honor their Child received inundated their hearts with the highest joy.

The Mother of God accepted everything most humbly and thankfully. Finally, the kings incensed the Child, Mary, Joseph, and the whole cave. (This was for them a ceremony expressing veneration.) Then they withdrew for the evening.

Afterward, the kings were in their tent reclining on a carpet around a little low table. Joseph brought in little plates of fruit, rolls, honeycomb, and small dishes of vegetables. Then he sat down and ate with them. He was so delighted, and though he wept for joy almost the whole time, he was not at all embarrassed by his tears.

When Joseph returned to the crib cave, he removed all the rich gifts of the kings to a recess at the right of the crib, where he had screened off a little corner from sight. Neither Mary nor Joseph examined the gifts or showed any worldly pleasure on their account. They were accepted with thanks, and with liberality they were again distributed to the needy.

On this evening and during the night, at first the only movement in Bethlehem was at Joseph's father's house, a noisy bustling back and forth. But when the kings entered the city, there was considerable excitement. Still, around the crib cave all was, at first, very quiet.

After a while, here and there in the distance people began gathering and whispering together, giving notice in the city of what they had seen. In Jerusalem on this day, many Jewish elders and priests were hurrying back and forth with writings to Herod. Then all became quiet as if they wished the subject to be dropped.

At last, the kings, with their retinue, held a religious service under the cedar by one of the caves. The singing was most touching, as the boys' sweet voices mingled with those of the elders. After the service, the kings went with some of their followers to a large inn at Bethlehem. The others slept in the tents between the crib and the cave.

On the next day, the kings again visited the crib cave separately. During the whole day, they gave away much of what they had brought, especially to the shepherds out in the field where their beasts had been sheltered. Poor old women bent with age went around with cloaks over their shoulders given them by the kings' generosity. The royal visitors must have already received a warning to reduce their luggage as much as possible on their return journey.

That evening, the kings came again to the crib cave, to say goodbye. One of them took the Child in his arms. He shed abundant tears, and his face was beaming with joy. Then followed the others, who departed with many tears after again offering numerous lavish gifts and a variety of food items.

The Blessed Virgin stood by them when they took their leave. The kings' gifts were received by Mary and Joseph with touching humility and sincere thanks to the donors, but without any indications of attachment. During the whole of this wonderful visit, Mary never showed the least shadow of self-interest. In her love for the Child Jesus and compassion for Joseph, she thought that the possession of these treasures would, perhaps, prevent their being treated in Bethlehem with the kind of contempt that had been shown them on their arrival. Joseph's trouble and humiliation on that account had been to her a source of suffering.

Lamps were already lighted in the crib cave when the kings departed. They went out behind the hill toward the east, to the field where their people and beasts were waiting. They all gathered together and prayed, singing with indescribable sweetness. Joseph entertained the kings again in the tent by the crib cave, and then they and their nobles returned to their inn at Bethlehem.

Meanwhile, the governor of the city (either acting on a secret order from Herod or moved by a spirit of presumption), had resolved to arrest the kings then in Bethlehem and to accuse them to Herod as disturbers of the peace. But an angel appeared in their sleep to the kings that night in Bethlehem and to their followers in their tents near the crib. He warned them to depart immediately and to hurry home by another way.

Those in the tents immediately awakened Joseph and told him the command just received. While they began to arouse the whole encampment and order the tents to be taken down—

which was done with incredible speed—Joseph hurried off to
Bethlehem to report it to the kings. But they, leaving most of
their baggage behind them, had already started out from the
city. Joseph met them on the way and told them why he had
come. They informed him that they, too, had received similar
instructions from an angel.

Their hurried departure went unnoticed in Bethlehem.
Leaving quietly and without their baggage, an observer might
have concluded that they were simply going to their servants,
perhaps for prayer. While they were still in the cave, weeping
and taking their leave, their followers were already starting
out in separate groups so they could travel more quickly. The
retinue hurried to the south, taking a route different from the
one by which they had come, through the desert of Ein Gedi
along the Dead Sea.

The kings begged the Holy Family to flee with them. When
Mary and Joseph refused, they begged Mary at least to conceal
herself with Jesus in the other cave so that she might not on
their account be harmed. They left many things to Joseph to
give away. The Blessed Virgin, taking the veil from her head,
gave it to them. She had been accustomed to swaddling the
Infant Jesus in its folds when holding Him in her arms.

The kings still held the Child in their arms one last time.
They were shedding tears and speaking quite touching words.
At last they gave their light silk cloaks to Mary, mounted their
camels, and hurried away. An angel was beside them in the
field, pointing out the way they should take. The caravan was
now much smaller, and the beasts were only lightly burdened.

Each king rode at about a quarter of an hour's distance from
the others. They seemed to have vanished all of a sudden. They
met again in a little city and then rode forward more slowly
than when they had left Bethlehem. The angel went always
before them, and sometimes spoke with them.

Mary, wrapping the Child Jesus in her cloak, at once withdrew
to the other cave. The gifts of the kings, and all that they had
left, were also taken there by the shepherds who had remained
around the encampment in the valley. The kings' people who had

preferred to remain behind their masters lent a helping hand. The three oldest of the shepherds, who had been the first to do homage to Jesus, received very rich presents from the kings.

When it was discovered in Bethlehem that the caravan had departed, the travelers were already near Ein Gedi. The valley where they had encamped was, with the exception of some tentpoles left standing and the footprints in the grass, as lonely and quiet as before.

The appearance of the royal caravan had caused great excitement in Bethlehem. Many now regretted that they had refused lodgings to Joseph. Some spoke of the kings and their followers as if they were a swarm of adventurers, while others connected their advent with the reports they had heard of the wonderful angelic appearances to the shepherds.

From the city hall a proclamation was made to the assembled citizens: namely, that they should beware of all preposterous opinions and superstitious reports, and go no more to the dwelling of those people outside the city. When the crowd had dispersed, Joseph was taken twice to the city hall. The second time, he took with him some of the gifts of the kings, which he presented to the Jewish elders who had taken him to task. Then he was let go.

There was another way leading from the city to the neighborhood of the crib cave. It was not by way of the city gate, but from that place where Mary, on the evening of her arrival with Joseph in Bethlehem, had rested under the tree while waiting for Joseph to find a lodging. This point of exit was blocked up by several people with a fallen tree. They also erected a watchhouse with a bell attached to a rope stretched across the road. In this way, anyone trying to take that route would soon be discovered.

About sixteen soldiers came to Joseph at the crib cave. But when they found only Mary and the Child with him, they returned to the city to report. Joseph had carefully concealed the royal gifts in other caves in the hill under the crib cave. No one knew of these caves but Joseph, who had discovered them long before in his boyhood. They had existed from the time of Jacob who, when Bethlehem consisted of only a couple of huts, had a tent there with his followers.

After the departure of the kings, the Holy Family moved over into the other cave, and the crib cave was left quite empty, with the donkey alone still standing there. Everything, even the hearth, had been cleared away. Mary was peaceful and happy in her new dwelling, which had been arranged somewhat comfortably. Her bed was near the wall, and by her rested the Child Jesus in an oval basket made of broad strips of bark.

The upper end of the basket, where the head of the Infant Jesus lay, was arched over with a cover. The basket itself stood on a woven partition, in front of which Mary sometimes sat with the Child beside her. Joseph had a separate space at a little distance.

Above the movable partition, there projected from the wall a pole to which a lamp was suspended. Joseph would bring in a pitcher of water and something in a dish. But he did not go any more to Bethlehem for necessities; the shepherds brought him all that he needed.

Many persons going up to Bethlehem for the Sabbath came to the crib cave. But when they no longer found Mary there, they went on to the city.

Mary and Joseph were full of devout feelings for the Child Jesus. But their expression of it was quite unaffected and simple, as is always the case among holy, chosen souls. The Child displayed a love in turning toward His mother that is by no means usual in young children.

Now there were again in Bethlehem soldiers searching in many houses for the newborn Child who had earlier been reported to Herod by the kings. They especially inconvenienced by their questions a noble Jewish lady who was in bed with her newborn child, but they did not return to the crib cave. It was now reported that only a poor, Jewish family had been there, but nothing more could be learned about them.

Two of the old shepherds went to Joseph (two of those who had first gone to the crib) and warned him about what was going on in Bethlehem. Then Joseph and Mary, with the Child Jesus, made their way from the cave to the tomb under the large cedar tree where the kings had sung one evening. It was about seven and a half minutes distant from the cave.

The tree stood upon a hill at whose foot lay a slanting door opening into a passage that led to a perpendicular door that closed the entrance to the tomb. The shepherds often stayed in the front part of it. In front of the tomb was a spring.

The tomb cave itself was not square, but rather rounded in form. At the upper end, which was somewhat broader, something like a scalloped stone coffin stood on heavy supports on a foundation of stone; you could see between it and the coffin. The interior of the cave was of soft, white stone.

The Holy Family entered the cave by night with a covered light. In the cave that they had vacated nothing now was to be seen that could attract notice. The beds had been rolled up and taken away, as well as all their household effects. It looked like an abandoned dwelling.

Some days later, some shepherds entered the tomb cave and spoke to Mary. They told her that government officials were coming to find her Child. Joseph hurried off with the Child Jesus wrapped in his cloak, and Mary, for half a day perhaps, sat in the cave very anxious and without the Child.

After Joseph returned, on the anniversary of Joseph and Mary's betrothal, a very beautiful ceremony was celebrated in the crib cave. With the help of the shepherds, Joseph had taken advantage of Mary's withdrawal to the tomb cave to adorn the whole interior of the crib cave. It was decorated with flower garlands, both walls and roof, and in the center stood a table.

All the beautiful carpets and fabrics of the kings that had not yet been removed were spread over the floor and hung in garlands from the walls. A cover was spread on the table, and on it was placed a pyramid of flowers and foliage that reached to the opening in the roof. On top of the pyramid hovered a dove. The whole cave was full of light and splendor.

The Child Jesus in His little basket cradle was placed on a stool on the table. He sat upright as He had done on the lap of His Mother at the adoration of the kings. Joseph and Mary were standing on either side of Him.

They were adorned with wreaths, and they drank something out of a glass. Choirs of angels filled the cave. All were very happy and full of emotion. When the celebration was over, the Holy Family immediately set about preparing for their departure. Their household goods had steadily diminished. The portable partitions and other pieces of furniture made by Joseph were now given to the shepherds, who removed them at once.

The Blessed Virgin went twice by night to the crib cave with the Child Jesus, laying Him on a carpet on the spot where He had been born. Then she knelt down at His side and prayed. The whole cave filled with light as it was at the moment of His birth.

The cave was now entirely cleared out. The other cave where the Holy Family had moved, as well as the crib cave, were now quite empty. They had also been swept out, for Joseph wanted to leave everything perfectly clean.

On the night before they departed for the Temple in Jerusalem, Mary and Joseph took leave of the crib cave with a kind of formal ceremony. They spread the deep red cover of the kings first over that spot where the Child Jesus was born, laid the Child on it, and kneeling beside Him, prayed. Then they laid the Child in the crib and again prayed beside Him. Finally, on the place where He had been circumcised, they also knelt in prayer.

Joseph had caused the young donkey to be pawned among his relatives because he was still resolved to return to Bethlehem and build himself a house in the valley of the shepherds. This intention he had mentioned to the shepherds. He told them he would take Mary for a while to her mother, so that she could recover from the hardships endured in her recent dwelling place. Then he left many items with them to be retrieved later.

Little did he know that he would never be able to carry out that plan.

# CHAPTER NINE

# THE PRESENTATION IN THE TEMPLE

BEFORE the break of day, Mary seated herself on the donkey, with the Child Jesus on her lap. She had only a couple of covers and one bundle. She sat on a side seat that had a little footboard. With Joseph, they started out around the crib hill and off by the east side of Bethlehem, unnoticed by anyone.

At midday they rested at a spring that was roofed in and surrounded by seats. A couple of women came out there to Mary, bringing to her little mugs and rolls. The food that the Holy Family had with them was hanging in a basket on the donkey. The basket had three compartments; two contained fruit, and in the third, which was of open wickerwork, were doves.

Toward evening, when they were about a quarter of an hour's distance from Jerusalem, they turned and entered a small house that lay next to a large inn. The owners were a married couple without children, and they welcomed the holy travelers with extraordinary joy. The husband was a gardener; he clipped the hedges and kept the road in order. The wife was a relative of Johanna, the wife of Chusa [Lk 8:2–3; 24:10].

They were Essenes. The couple did out of pure love all they could for the Mother of God. They must have had some intuition of the Child's holiness.

The whole of the next day, the Holy Family still remained with the old couple outside Jerusalem. The Blessed Virgin was almost all the time alone in her room with the Child, who lay upon a low, covered projection of the wall. She was always in prayer, and she appeared to be preparing herself for the purification sacrifice. In her room myriads of angels adored the Child Jesus. Mary was wholly absorbed in her own interior thoughts.

In Jerusalem lived the priest Simeon. He was a very aged, emaciated man with a short beard. He had a wife and three grown sons, the youngest of whom was already twenty years old.

Simeon lived at the Temple. He used to go through a narrow, dark passage in the wall of the Temple to a little cell that was built in the thick walls. It had only one opening, from which he could look down into the Temple.

Here the old man knelt and prayed in ecstasy. An angel appeared before him, telling him to notice particularly the first Child that would, early the next morning, be brought for presentation. For that Child was the Messiah whom he had now awaited so long. The angel added that, after seeing the Child, he would die.

It was a beautiful sight: The little cell was so bright, and the old man so radiant with joy. He went home full of gladness, announced to his wife the good news of the angel, and then returned to his prayer. Anna, an elderly widow who lived in a Temple cell, was also rapt in prayer, and she, too, had a vision.

Early in the morning while it was still quite dark, the Holy Family went into the city and to the Temple accompanied by the old couple. The donkey was heavily loaded as if for a journey, and they had with them the basket of offerings. They first entered a court that was surrounded by a wall, and there the donkey was tied under a shed.

The Blessed Virgin and Child were received by an old woman and led along a covered walk up to the Temple. The old woman carried a light, for it was still dark. Here in this passage came Simeon, full of expectation to meet Mary.

He spoke a few joyous words with her, took the Child Jesus, pressed Him to his heart, and then hurried to another side of the Temple. Since the previous evening, when he had received the announcement of the angel, he had been consumed by the desire to see the Child. He had taken his stand in the women's passage to the Temple, hardly able to await the coming of Mary and her Child.

The beautiful ceremony of presentation took place around an altar where the infant Jesus was laid in a basket cradle, alongside the offerings. When the most holy Child Jesus was laid on the altar in the basket cradle, an indescribable light filled the Temple. God was in that light, and the heavens opened up all the way to the Most Holy Trinity.

Several priests took part in the ceremony. One of them took the Child from the cradle, then lifted Him upward and toward the different parts of the Temple, praying all the while. Simeon next received the Child from him, laid the Babe in Mary's arms, and prayed over her and the Child with words from a roll of parchment that lay near him on a desk.

Finally, two priests at the altar began a religious service accompanied by incense and prayers. When these ceremonies were ended, Simeon walked to where Mary was standing, took the Child into his arms and, entranced with joy, spoke long and loudly. When he finished, Anna was also filled with the Spirit and spoke a long time, as the Gospel tells us [Lk 2:25–38].

Mary shone like a rose. Her public offerings were indeed the poorest, but Joseph in private gave to Simeon and to Anna many little, yellow, triangular coins for the Temple's use. They were intended primarily for the maidens belonging to it who were too poor to meet their own expenses.

Other children were presented at the Temple that day. All the children offered on that day received special grace, and some of them were among the infants of Bethlehem who were to be martyred.

Mary was now led back into the court by Anna and Noemi (Mary's former governess). Here she left them and was joined by Joseph and the old couple with whom she and Joseph had lodged. They went with the donkey straight out of Jerusalem, and the good couple accompanied them a part of the way. They reached a small village the same day and stayed overnight in the house that had been Mary's last stopping place on her journey to the Temple many years before. Here some of Anne's people were waiting to lead them home.

After prophesying in the Temple, Simeon returned home and fell sick. On his bed he gave his last advice to his wife and sons, and imparted to them his joy. Then he died, with several Jewish elders and priests praying around him.

The Holy Family returned to Nazareth by a much more direct route than the one they had taken to Bethlehem. On their first journey, they had avoided the inhabited districts and seldom put up at an inn. But now they took the straight route, which was much shorter.

Joseph had in his cloak pocket some little rolls of thin, yellow, shining leaves of gold on which were inscribed letters. He had received them from the holy kings.

Finally they arrived at Anne's house in Nazareth. A feast was held like the one that had been celebrated when the child Mary had departed for the Temple. Lamps burned above the table, and there were some old priests present.

At the feast, things went quietly. Though there was great joy over the Child Jesus, yet it was a calm, inward joy, with no agitation in those holy souls. They partook of a small meal, with the women as usual eating apart from the men.

The journey from Anne's house to Joseph's in Nazareth took about half an hour. The road ran between gardens and hills. At Anne's house, Joseph loaded two donkeys with many different items, then went on ahead with Anne's maid to Nazareth. Mary followed with Anne, who carried the Child Jesus.

Mary and Joseph had no housekeeping responsibilities in those days. They were provided with all they needed by Anne, who often went to see them. Her maid carried provisions to them in two baskets, one on her head, the other in her hand.

The Blessed Virgin spent much of her time knitting and crocheting little robes for Jesus. She worked standing or sitting by the Child, who lay in His little basket cradle. Meanwhile, Joseph used long strips of bark—yellow, brown, and green—to plait screens, large surfaces, and covers for ceilings. He wove into them all kinds of patterns: stars, hearts, and more.

Joseph had a stock of this woven board-like work piled under a shed near the house. Little did he realize that soon he would have to leave it all.

# CHAPTER TEN

# THE FLIGHT INTO EGYPT

W HEN Herod saw that the kings did not return, he thought they had failed to find Jesus, and the whole affair seemed to be dying out. But after Mary's return to Nazareth, Herod heard of Simeon's and Anna's prophecies at the presentation of the Child in the Temple, and his fears were reawakened. He was stirred up into a state of anxiety as great as he had known when the kings came to Jerusalem.

Herod was conferring with some aged Jewish elders who read to him from long scrolls mounted on rods. He had given orders for a number of men to be gathered together in a large court and provided there with weapons and uniforms. He then sent these troops to various places around Jerusalem.

From these places the mothers were to be summoned to the Holy City. He caused their numbers to be determined everywhere. Herod took these precautions to prevent the tumult that would necessarily follow if the news of the projected slaughter of the children was spread.

Those soldiers were stationed in three different places: Bethlehem, Gilgal, and Hebron. The inhabitants were in great distress because they could not understand why a garrison was placed in their towns. The soldiers remained about nine months in those places, before the murder of the little ones began.

At this time, Anne was still at the home of the Holy Family in Nazareth. Mary, with her Child (who was then twelve weeks old), slept in the apartment to the right behind the fireplace; Anne, to the left. These rooms were not as high as the house itself and were separated only by wicker partitions. The ceiling also was of wickerwork.

Mary's bed was surrounded by a curtain. At her feet, in His own little bed, lay the Infant Jesus within Mary's reach when she sat upright.

One night an angel appearing as a radiant youth stood at the side of Joseph's bed and spoke to him. Joseph sat up, but overcome by sleep, again lay down. Then the youth caught him by the hand and raised him up, saying: "Rise, take the Child and His mother, and flee to Egypt, for Herod is about to search for the Child, to destroy Him" [Mt 2:13].

Joseph, now thoroughly awakened, stood up, and the youth vanished. Then Joseph went to the lamp that burned in the center of the house and got a light. He proceeded to Mary's chamber, knocked, and asked permission to enter.

He went in and spoke to her, then went out to the stable for the donkey. Returning, he went into a room where all kinds of household goods were stored. He was getting things ready for a journey. Mary arose, quickly clothed herself for travelling, and went to rouse Anne.

Anne was deeply distressed. She embraced Mary over and over again with many tears, clasping her to her heart as if she were never again to see her.

Only just before setting out did they take the infant Jesus from His little bed. They all pressed the Child to their heart. Mary then took the Child upon her breast, resting Him in a strip of cloth that fastened over her shoulders.

A long cloak enveloped both Mother and Child, and Mary wore over her head a large veil, which hung down on both sides of her face. She made only a few preparations for the journey, and all she did was done quietly and quickly.

The holy travelers took only a few things with them, far fewer than they had brought from Bethlehem, only a little bundle and some coverings. Joseph had a leather bottle filled with water and a basket with compartments in it, in which were loaves, little jugs, and live birds. There was a cross seat for Mary and the Child on the donkey, as well as a little footboard.

They went forward a short distance with Anne, for they took the road in the direction to her house. When Joseph approached with the donkey, Anne again embraced and blessed Mary, who then mounted and rode off. It was not yet midnight when they left the house. Anne then packed up everything in Joseph's house for her husband and a servant to move her to her home.

The Holy Family passed by many places that night. Not till morning did they rest in a shed and take a little refreshment. They made their first night's lodgings in a little village whose poor, oppressed people were not, properly speaking, Jews. They had to go far over a mountainous road to Samaria to worship, for their temple was on Mount Gerizim, and they always had to work like slaves on the Temple of Jerusalem and other public buildings.

The Holy Family could go no farther. They were well received by these outcasts, remaining with them the whole of the following day. On their later return from Egypt, they again visited these poor people. They did the same both going and returning from the Temple the first time that the Child Jesus made the journey there. The whole family at a later period was baptized by John, and they afterward joined the disciples of Jesus.

As they fled to Egypt, the three holy travelers came to only three inns where they could spend the night: here, among the oppressed Samaritans; at a second place among camel dealers; and in a third settlement among robbers. Ironically, the more "respectable" people seemed to reject them. Everywhere else, they had to rest during their tiresome wanderings in valleys and caves and the most out-of-the-way places.

Some distance from the village of the outcasts, they hid under the great pine tree near the place where Mary, on their journey to Bethlehem, had been so cold. The persecution of Herod was known in these parts, so it was unsafe for them. The Ark of the Covenant had once rested under this tree, when Joshua assembled the people and made them renounce their idols.

Later, the Holy Family came to a well and balsam bush. There they rested and refreshed themselves. The branches of the bush were notched, and out of them oozed the balsam in drops. The Child Jesus lay on Mary's lap, with His little feet bare. Behind them lay Jerusalem far up above the level of the country where they were then.

When the Holy Family had passed the walls of Gaza, they came to the wilderness. No words can depict the difficulties of this journey. They always traveled a mile east of the ordinary highway and, since they avoided the public inns, they suffered the lack of all necessities.

At one place, quite exhausted with not a drop of water (the little jug was empty), they drew close to a low bush some distance from the road. The Blessed Virgin got down from the donkey and sat down upon the dry grass. Suddenly there sprang up high before them a spring of water, which spread over the plain. They rejoiced at the miracle.

Joseph dug a hole at a little distance and led the donkey to it. The poor beast gladly drank from it as it filled. Mary bathed the Child in the spring and refreshed herself. The sun shone out beautifully for a short time, and the weary travelers were strengthened and full of gratitude. They remained here for two or three hours.

On the sixth night, they came to a cave near the mount and city of Ephraim. The cave was in a wild ravine, about an hour's distance from the oaks of Mamre [Gn 18:1]. The Holy Family arrived worn-out and dejected. Mary was very sad; she wept, for they were in need of everything.

They rested here a whole day, and many wonders were granted them for their refreshment. A spring gushed forth in the cave; a wild goat came running to them and allowed itself to be milked. They were even visibly consoled by an angel.

One of the prophets had often prayed in this cave. Samuel had once stayed there while traveling. David had guarded his father's sheep around it and had often withdrawn to pray there. In this cave, he had received through angels the commands of God, among them the command to slay Goliath.

The last stopping place of the Holy Family in Herod's dominion was near its borders. The innkeepers appeared to be camel dealers, for a number of camels were grazing in an enclosed pasture ground. The people were rude and wild, and they enriched themselves by thievery. Still, they received the Holy Family most graciously. This place was a couple of hours' travel from the Dead Sea.

Mary sent a messenger to Elizabeth, who then brought her child, young John, to a well-concealed place in the desert. Zachary accompanied her only a part of the way. When they reached a certain body of water, Elizabeth and the child crossed over on a raft, while Zachary went on to Nazareth by the same route Mary had taken on her visit to Elizabeth. He was going to make some inquiries, for there were some friends at Nazareth who were distressed at Mary's departure.

One starry night, the Holy Family crossed a sandy wilderness covered with low thickets. Here and there under the dense growth, venomous snakes lay coiled. With loud hissing, they approached the path and darted their heads angrily toward the travelers.

But Mary, Jesus, and Joseph, shielded by the light that surrounded them, walked securely along. Other animals surrounded them as well, with immense fins like wings on their black bodies, with short feet, and heads like that of a fish. They darted along, flying over the ground.

At last, the Holy Family made their way past the bushes to a deep crevice in the ground, like the walls of a narrow gorge. Here they rested.

In the last place in Judea they passed by, the people were very rude and uncivilized. The Holy Family could get nothing from them for refreshment. Leaving this last place and scarcely knowing how to proceed, they pressed on through a desolate region.

The travelers could find no road, and a dark, pathless mountain height stretched out before them. Mary was exhausted and very sad. She knelt with Joseph, the Child in her arms, and cried out to God.

Suddenly, several large, wild beasts, like lions, came running around them, showing themselves friendly. They had been sent by God to show the way. They looked toward the mountain, ran there, and then turned back again, just like a dog that wants someone to follow it. At last the Holy Family understood their intention and followed them and, after crossing the mountain, they arrived at a very dismal region.

At some distance from the road where they were travelling, a light glimmered through the darkness. It shone from a hut belonging to a gang of robbers who had hung a light on a neighboring tree to entice travelers. Here and there, the road was broken by pits over which cords with little bells were stretched. The ringing of these bells alerted the robbers to the presence of luckless wayfarers.

Suddenly, a man with about five comrades surrounded the Holy Family. All were motivated by wicked intentions. But when they looked at the Child, a glittering ray like an arrow penetrated the heart of the leader, who immediately commanded his comrades to do no harm to the strangers. (Mary also saw the ray.) The robber now took the Holy Family to his home and told his wife how strangely his heart had been moved.

The people were at first shy and ashamed, something very unusual for them. Still, they approached, little by little, and gathered around Mary, Jesus, and Joseph, who had seated themselves in a corner on the ground. Some of the men went in and out, while the woman brought to Mary little rolls, fruits, honeycomb, and cups containing something to drink. The donkey also was placed under shelter.

The woman cleared out a small room for Mary and brought her a little tub of water to bathe the Child. She also dried the swaddling bands for her at the fire. The husband was deeply impressed by the demeanor of the Holy Family, and especially the appearance of the Child.

He said to his wife, "This Hebrew Child is no ordinary child. Beg the Lady to allow us to wash our leprous child in His bathing water. It may, perhaps, do it some good."

The wife went to request the favor of the Blessed Virgin. But before she had time to speak, Mary told her to take the water she had used for Jesus's bath and wash the sick child in it. He would become even cleaner, she said, than he was before he contracted the disease.

The boy was about three years old and stiff from leprosy. His mother carried him in and put him into the bath. Wherever the water touched him, the leprosy fell like scales to the bottom of the tub. The boy became clean and well.

His mother was beside herself with joy. Mary told her to dig a hole deep down to a rock and pour the water just used into it. That way she could always have it for similar purposes. Mary spoke with her a long time and obtained from her a promise to take the first opportunity to escape from the dangers of her present home.

The people were all delighted. They stood around the Holy Family, gazing at them in wonder. During the night, other members of their band came to the hut, and they were told about the boy's cure.

The robbers' reverence toward the Holy Family was even more remarkable, given that the very same night many travelers, attracted to their hut by the light, were immediately taken prisoner by the travelers and were carried deep into the forest to an immense cave to be kept captive. It lay under a thicket, with the entrance closely concealed.

In it were clothes, carpets, meat, goats, sheep, and innumerable other stolen things, all in abundance. There were also boys about seven or eight years old whom the robbers had kidnapped. They were cared for by an old woman who lived in the cave.

Mary slept none at all that night. She sat upon her bed on the floor perfectly still. At early dawn the Holy Family started again on their journey in spite of the robber and his wife, who wanted them to stay longer.

She and Joseph took with them a supply of provisions put up by their grateful host and hostess. The couple also accompanied them a part of the way, so that they might escape the snares. The robber and his wife took leave of the Holy Family with expressions of deep emotion, uttering these remarkable words: "Remember us wherever you go!"

The cured boy afterward turned out to be the Good Thief who on the cross said to Jesus: "Remember me when You come into Your kingdom!" [see Lk 23:42]. The robber's wife, after some time, left him and joined those who lived around the balsam garden.

The Holy Family went from here farther out into the desert. When they had again lost all trace of anything like a path, they were a second time surrounded by all kinds of animals, among them huge winged lizards and even serpents. These beasts pointed out the way to them.

At a later time, when they were unable to move forward through a sandy plain, a very lovely miracle took place. On either side of the road sprouted up the plant called Rose of Jericho, with its crisped branches, its tiny flowers in the center, and its straight root. On they went now quite joyously, watching as far as the eye could see these plants springing up, all across the whole plain. It was revealed to the Blessed Virgin that, at some future day, the people of the country would gather these roses and sell them to travelers in exchange for bread.

The Holy Family next arrived at a town where there were numerous canals and ditches with high dams. They crossed the water on a raft. Mary sat on a log, and the donkey was standing in something like a tub. Two men ferried them over.

Our holy travelers came now to a house on the outskirts of town. But the occupants were so rough and pitiless that, without saying a word, Mary and Joseph moved farther on. This was the first pagan Egyptian city they had yet reached. They had made, up to this time, ten days' journey in the country of the Jews and then in the wilderness.

Next the Holy Family crossed through Egyptian territory, in a level, green country full of pasture grounds. In the trees were stationed idols like swaddled dolls and fishes wrapped in broad bands inscribed with figures and letters. Occasionally, people who were fat but short in stature approached these idols and venerated them.

The three travelers sought a little rest in a cattle shed, with the cattle moving out on their own accord to make room for them. They were in need of food, having neither bread nor water. Mary no longer had nourishment for her Child, and no one gave them anything. Every type of human misery was experienced by them during this journey.

At last, some shepherds came near to water their cattle. They, too, would have gone away without giving them anything had not Joseph's pleas moved them to unlock the well and allow them to have a little water.

Next, the Holy Family came to a forest, still weary and exhausted. At its edge stood a slender date tree with the fruit all clustered on top. Mary approached the tree, with the Child Jesus on her arm, praying and lifting the Child up to it.

Instantly the tree bowed down its top as if kneeling so that Mary could gather all its fruit. It afterward remained in that position. Mary divided a quantity of the fruit among the naked children who had run after them from the last village.

At a quarter of an hour's distance from this date tree stood another unusually large one. It was quite tall, and hollow like an old oak. In it the Holy Family lay hidden from the people who followed them. That evening they took shelter within the walls of a nearby ruined place, where they stayed overnight.

On the following day, the Holy Family continued their journey through another sandy, desolate wilderness. Thirsting for water and exhausted by weariness, they sat down on one of the sandhills, and the Blessed Virgin sent up a cry to God. Suddenly, a stream of pure water gushed forth at her side.

Joseph removed the sandhill that was over it, and a clear, beautiful, little fountain jetted up. He made a channel for it, and it flowed over quite a large space, disappearing again near its source. Here they refreshed themselves, and Mary bathed the Child Jesus, while Joseph gave drink to the donkey and filled the water bottles. All kinds of animals such as turtles came to drink at the gushing waters. They did not appear at all afraid of the Holy Family.

The soil over which the water had flowed soon began to clothe itself with green growth. Numerous balsam trees afterward grew there. When the Holy Family returned from Egypt, those trees were large enough to furnish balsam for their refreshment. The place soon grew into a little settlement.

Wherever the Gentiles planted these trees, they withered. They thrived only when the Jews whom the Holy Family had known in this country went to live there. The wife of that robber whose boy had been cured of leprosy by the bath of the Child Jesus went there, too, for she soon escaped from the robbers. Her boy, however, remained with them some time longer.

## ⊰ CHAPTER ELEVEN ⊱

## *LIFE IN EGYPT*

FINALLY, Jesus, Mary, and Joseph made their way to the Egyptian city of Heliopolis. From their previous night lodging, they were accompanied there by a good man who was one of the workmen on that canal over which they had been ferried. They now crossed a long and very high bridge over the Nile River that appeared to have several branches, and they came to a place before the city gate that was surrounded by a kind of promenade.

Here on a tapering pedestal stood a great idol with the head of an ox, and in its arms something like the figure of a swaddled child. The idol was encircled by tables of stone on which the worshippers laid their sacrifices. Not far off was a very large tree where the Holy Family sat down to rest.

They had scarcely seated themselves when the earth began to quake. The idol tottered and tilted over. A loud outcry instantly arose from the people, and many of the workmen on the canal in the neighborhood came rushing up. But the good man who had accompanied the Holy Family started with them toward the city. They were already at the opposite side of the idol place when the terrified crowd, with menacing and abusive words, angrily surrounded them.

Suddenly the earth heaved and the huge tree fell, its roots breaking up out of the ground. There arose a lake of muddy water into which the idol splashed. It sank so deep that one could scarcely see its horns, and some of the most wicked of the bystanders sank with it.

The Holy Family now entered the city unhindered, and they took up lodging near an idolatrous temple, a large stone building containing many rooms. Some of the idols in the temples of the city were in the same way overturned.

Heliopolis was a great city that extended far beyond the many-branched river. The Holy Family lived there under a low colonnade where there were other dwellings besides their own. The supporting pillars were rather low, some round, some square, and above ran a highway to accommodate vehicles and pedestrians. Opposite this colonnade was a pagan temple with two courts.

Joseph set up before their little dwelling a screen of light woodwork. There was room for the donkey as well. The screen that Joseph put up was of the same kind as he was accustomed to making. Behind a similar screen, set up against the wall, he placed an altar consisting of a small table covered with red cloth, and over that a white, transparent cloth; on it stood a lamp.

While they lived here, Joseph worked both at home and abroad. He made long rods with round knobs at the ends, little three-legged stools with a handle for grasping them, and a certain kind of basket. He made as well a great many light wicker partitions and little light towers, some hexagonal, others octagonal.

The towers were formed of long, thin boards, tapering toward the top and ending in a knob. They had an entrance and were large enough to allow someone to occupy them as if they were sentry boxes. They had steps outside where they could be mounted.

Little towers like these were standing here and there before the pagan temples, as well as on the flat roofs of the houses.

People used to sit in them. Perhaps they were watch houses, or maybe they were intended as screens from the sun.

The Blessed Virgin spent much of her time weaving tapestry and doing other kinds of work with fabric. People often visited her and the little Infant Jesus.

The Child lay on the ground by Mary's side, in a kind of cradle like a little boat. Sometimes it was raised on a frame like a sawing-jack. There were not many Jews in Heliopolis; they went about with a downcast look as if others thought they had no right to live there.

North of Heliopolis, between it and the Nile (which divides there into several branches), lay the little territory of Goshen. In it was a little place cut up by canals where there lived numerous Jews whose religious ideas were very much confused. Several of them became acquainted with the Holy Family, and Mary did all kinds of work for them, receiving as payment bread and other provisions. The Jews in the Land of Goshen had a temple, which they presumptuously compared with the Temple of Solomon, but the two temples were very different.

Not far from his dwelling, Joseph built a place of prayer where the resident Jews, who possessed no such place of their own, used to assemble with the Holy Family for prayer. A light cupola on top could be thrown open, enabling the worshippers to stand under the open sky. In the center of the hall stood an altar, covered as usual with red and white. On it lay rolls of parchment. The priest, their rabbi, was a very old man. The men and women were not as far separated from one another at prayer as in Palestine; the men stood on one side and the women on the other.

The Holy Family remained a little more than a year at Heliopolis. They had much to suffer from the Egyptians, who hated and persecuted them, because of the overturned idols. Since the houses were all solidly built, Joseph could not find much work at his trade. For all these reasons, they finally left Heliopolis.

By this time, Herod had summoned to Jerusalem the mothers of Bethlehem, Gilgal, and Hebron with their boys, from infants in the arms up to the age of two years. They were rounded up in a large building with a courtyard. Inside, the children were forcibly taken from their mothers by soldiers and carried out into the courtyard. Herod was in the upper story in a great hall, where he could look out a window to watch his brutal commands being carried out.

In the courtyard, about twenty other soldiers were fiendishly at work with swords and lances, piercing the little creatures through throat and heart. The little bodies were slung together in a heap. When the mothers inside realized their children's horrible fate, they screamed, tore their hair, and clung to one another.

The slaughter lasted till near evening, and the bodies of the murdered children were at last buried together in a great pit in the courtyard. The mothers were held in chains that night, then taken back to their homes by the soldiers. Similar scenes were enacted in other places, for the massacre was carried on during several days.

Before the Holy Family left Heliopolis, they learned from an angel of this terrible slaughter of the babies in Bethlehem. Both Mary and Joseph were deeply grieved. Even the Child Jesus, who was now able to walk (being a year and a half old), shed tears the whole day.

When they left the city, they took byroads and went still farther into the country, journeying southward toward Memphis. Passing through a little town not far from Heliopolis, they stopped in the forecourt of an open, pagan temple. There they sat down to rest.

Suddenly, down tumbled the idol and fell to pieces. It had the head of an ox with triple horns, and several cavities in the body to receive the sacrifices that were to be consumed. At once a tumult arose among the pagan priests; they seized the Holy Family and threatened them with punishment.

One of them told his companions, however, as they were consulting what measures to take, that the best thing for them to do would be to commend themselves to the God of these strangers. He remembered, he said, what plagues had come upon their Egyptian forefathers when they had persecuted those people, and that on the night of their departure from Egypt the firstborn in every house had died.

These words were effective, and the Holy Family was left in peace. The pagan priest who had spoken for them moved soon after with several of his people to another village. Mary, Jesus, and Joseph would eventually settle in that village, and he joined them and the Jewish community there.

Mary and Joseph next traveled with Jesus to a town on the eastern side of the Nile, opposite Memphis. It was large and very dirty. They had some intention of remaining there, but they were not well received. In fact, they could not get even a drink of water from the residents, much less the few dates for which they begged.

The holy travelers proceeded northward from there along the river toward the Egyptian town of Babylon, a dirty, low-lying city. Between the Nile and Babylon, they took the route by which they had come and returned a distance of about two hours. Buildings in ruins were scattered here and there along the whole road.

After crossing a small branch of the river, they reached a village built on a tongue of land jutting out into the Nile. The river bathed the city on two sides. It was, in general, a wretched enough place, built only of date-wood and solid mud covered with rushes.

Even so, Joseph found plenty of work here. He built more substantial houses of wickerwork with galleries around them. There, the occupants could go for air and recreation.

Here the Holy Family lived in a dark, vaulted cave that lay in a remote spot on the land side, not far from the gate by which they had entered. Joseph built a light screen in front of it, as he had with the cave at Heliopolis. One of the idols in a little temple fell at their arrival, and later all the others did the same.

The people were dismayed, but one of the priests quieted them by reminding them of the plagues of Egypt. After some time, as a little community of Jews and converted pagans gathered around the Holy Family, the priests gave over to them the little temple whose idol had fallen at their coming. Joseph turned it into a synagogue.

Joseph was like the patriarch of the community. He taught them how to sing the Psalms correctly, for Judaism in those parts had greatly deteriorated. Only the poorest Jews dwelt in this area, and those in the most wretched dens and caves.

In the nearby Jewish settlement between the village of On and the Nile, however, they were numerous and better off. They had a regular temple, which they said was like Solomon's temple. But that was idle boasting, for it was utterly different.

They no longer sang the Psalms, and they had lapsed into frightful idolatry. They had a golden calf and a figure with an ox's head, around which were arranged other representations of animals such as ferrets. These last animals were revered because they defended people against the Egyptian mongoose.

They also had an imitation of the Ark of the Covenant with obscene things in it. The idolatry they practiced was of the most shameful kind and, in a subterranean hall, they carried on the most infamous wickedness, deluded by the hope that from it their messiah would come forth. They were exceedingly stiff-necked and would not be converted.

In this place the Holy Family at first suffered greatly from need. Good water could not be had, and wood failed. The inhabitants used only dried grass and reeds for their cooking. Joseph, Mary, and Jesus usually had to eat cold food.

In time, however, Joseph had plenty to do. He improved the poor huts for the people, but they treated him almost like a slave, giving him for his labor only what they themselves thought appropriate. Sometimes he brought home something as a remuneration for his work, and sometimes he brought nothing.

The people were very unskillful in building their huts. They had no wood, except here and there a log or two. Even if they had had wood, they had no tools to shape it, for they had only knives of bone or stone. Joseph had brought the most necessary tools with him.

The Holy Family were soon settled somewhat comfortably. They had little stools and tables, wicker screens, and a well-ordered fireplace as well. Like the Egyptians, they ate sitting flat on the ground.

In the wall of Mary's sleeping area was a recess that Joseph had hollowed out, and in it was Jesus's little bed. Mary's bed was beside it, and often at night she knelt in prayer to God beside that little bed. Joseph slept in another enclosed corner.

The place of prayer for the Holy Family was in a passage outside the cave. Joseph and the Blessed Virgin had separate places in it, and Jesus, too, had His little corner, where He prayed sitting, standing, or kneeling. There was a kind of little altar in front of the Blessed Virgin's place, a small table covered with red and white.

This table was like a leaf on hinges that could be let down from the wall or raised up against it. When let down, it revealed a shelf in the wall itself. On the shelf were various objects, including a withered, though still whole, branch. On its top was the lily that had blossomed in Joseph's hand when he had been chosen by lot in the Temple for Mary's spouse.

At this point, the Holy Family had to subsist on fruit and bad water. They had been so long without good water that Joseph resolved to saddle the donkey, take his leather bottle, and set out for the balsam spring in the desert just to get some. But while the Blessed Virgin was praying, an angel appeared to her and told her that she should search for and find a spring at the back of their present dwelling.

She walked over the hill where they lived, to a deep, vacant lot that lay at some distance between ruined walls. A large, old tree stood on that ground. Mary had in her hand a rod with a little scoop attached, such as the people of that country commonly carry on journeys. She stuck it into the ground near the tree, and a beautiful, clear stream of water instantly gushed forth.

Mary hurried back joyfully to call Joseph. He soon removed the upper crust of earth and revealed a well that had long ago been dug out and lined with masonry, but which for some time had been choked up and dry. He soon restored it and paved it around very beautifully with stones.

At the side of the well where Mary had approached it lay a great stone almost like an altar. It had been used for that purpose in earlier times. After that, the Blessed Virgin often washed Jesus's clothes and bands of cloth here, then dried them in the sun.

This time of exile in Egypt was terribly burdensome to Joseph. He felt great sorrow to see the worship of idols, and to know that the Egyptians had abandoned the knowledge of the true God who, incarnate in the Child Jesus, was actually there among them. It also grieved him to see the contempt and ill treatment that many wicked people showed the Holy Family, and especially the way the Blessed Virgin suffered from that evil. Without a doubt, it was an extremely heavy cross for him to bear.

During one of the conversations of Mary and Joseph about the mysteries of the Lord, the Infant Jesus resolved to break the silence and speak in plain words to Joseph, who so faithfully fulfilled the duties of a foster father. The two holy spouses were speaking of the infinite being of God, of His goodness and abundant love, which led Him to send His only-begotten Son as the Teacher and Savior of the human race, clothing Him in human form so that He might converse with them and suffer the punishments of their depraved natures. Joseph was lost in wonder at the works of the Lord and inflamed by affectionate gratitude and exaltation of the Lord.

Seizing upon this occasion, the infant God, resting in the arms of His mother as upon the seat of wisdom, began to speak to Joseph in an intelligible voice, saying: "My father, I came from heaven to this earth to be the Light of the world, and to rescue it from the darkness of sin; to seek and know my sheep as a good Shepherd, to give them nourishment for eternal life, to teach them the way of heaven, and to open its gates, which had been closed by their sins. I desire that you both be children of the Light, which you have so close at hand."

These words of the Infant Jesus, being full of divine life, filled the heart of the patriarch Joseph with new love, reverence, and joy. He fell on his knees before the infant God with the most profound humility and thanked Him for having called him "father" by the very first word spoken to him. He sought the Lord with many tears to enlighten him and enable him to fulfill entirely His most holy will, to teach him to be thankful for the incomparable benefits flowing from His generous hands.

The well remained unknown and was used only by the Holy Family until Jesus had grown large enough to go on little errands and even to bring water for His mother. When the Boy Jesus brought water from the well for His mother for the first time, she was in prayer. He had slipped away with a bottle and brought it back full of water. Mary was unspeakably upset when she saw Him coming back with the water.

She knelt down and begged Him never to do that again, for He might fall into the well. But Jesus replied that He would be careful. He wanted to render her that service whenever she needed it.

Once He took other children to the well and gave them a drink of the water, which He scooped up in a hollow, crooked leaf. The little ones told this to their parents, so the well became known. Others then began to go to it, though it continued to be used primarily by the Jewish community. Even in the time of the Holy Family, it possessed healing properties for lepers.

As He grew, Jesus was eager to serve Joseph as well as Mary. If the carpenter happened to be working at a little distance from home, and left a tool behind, the Boy Jesus would run to get it and bring it to him. The Boy noticed everything. The joy that Mary and Joseph experienced on His account outweighed all their sufferings.

Though perfectly childlike, Jesus was very wise, and skilled in everything. He knew and understood everything. Mary and Joseph were often filled with unspeakable admiration for Him.

When the Boy Jesus took to their owners the covers embroidered or woven by His mother, who hoped to receive bread in return for her work, they teased Him at first. That made Him sad. But after a while, the Holy Family was very much loved by the people.

Other children would give Jesus figs and dates, while many of their elders would seek out the Holy Family for help and consolation. Everyone in trouble said, "Let's go to the Jewish Child."

Jesus went on all kinds of errands, even to a Jewish town a mile distant, to get bread in exchange for His mother's work. The wild animals, numerous on His route, did Him no harm. On the contrary, they and even the snakes showed Him affection.

Once He went with other children to the Jewish town; He was weeping bitterly over the degradation of the Jewish people. When He went for the first time alone to that town, He wore, also for the first time, the brown robe woven by Mary. It was trimmed around the border with yellow flowers.

Jesus knelt and prayed on the way. Two angels appeared to Him and spoke of Herod's death. But He said nothing of it to His parents.

# ❧ CHAPTER TWELVE ❧

## *THE RETURN TO NAZARETH*

EVEN long after Herod died, danger still threatened in the Holy Family's homeland, and they thought they could not return. But Joseph, who was always busy at his trade, grew deeply troubled one evening. The people for whom he had been working had given him nothing, so he had nothing to take home where there was so much need.

He knelt down in the open air and prayed. He was greatly afflicted. His journey among these pagan people was becoming intolerable.

They practiced abominable idolatry, even sacrificing deformed children. The parent that sacrificed a healthy, well-formed child was thought to be very pious. They had, besides, still more shameful rites that they carried on in secret. Even the Jews in the Jewish towns were to Joseph objects of horror; they could no longer be recognized as Jews, so deeply were they sunk in idolatry.

In his trouble he prayed to God for help, and an angel appeared to him. The heavenly visitor told him to arise and on the following morning depart from Egypt by the public high road. The angel also told him not to fear, for he would accompany him.

Joseph hurried with the news to the Blessed Virgin and Jesus. They all set to work right away to get their few movable belongings packed together on the donkeys. The next morning, with their intention to depart having become known, crowds of sorrowing neighbors came to them, bringing with them all kinds of gifts in little vessels of bark.

Several mothers brought their children. There was among them a noble lady with a little boy several years old. She called him Mary's son, because even though years before she had abandoned the hope of conceiving a boy, this child had been granted to her in response to Mary's prayer. This lady gave to the Boy Jesus triangular coins: yellow, white, and brown. Her little son was later on admitted by Jesus into the number of His disciples; he was named Deodatus.

The people of the place, more of them pagans than Jews, were sincerely grieved at the Holy Family's departure, though a few were glad. These last looked upon them as sorcerers who obtained all they desired through the help of Lucifer, the prince of devils.

Joseph, Mary, and Jesus then started out, accompanied by all their friends. They headed first to the balsam garden, because they wanted to rest there awhile and replenish their water supply. By then, the garden was already flourishing.

The balsam trees were as tall as moderately large grapevines and in four rows surrounded the garden, which had an entrance. There were sycamores and all kinds of fruit trees, some like dates. The spring sent a stream around the whole garden.

The friends that had accompanied them now left them, but the Holy Family remained for some hours. Joseph had made some little vessels out of bark; they were covered with pitch, very smooth and finely built. He snapped from the red balsam twigs the clover-like leaves and hung the flasks underneath in order to gather the balsam drops for the journey. When they stopped to rest, he often made, for their ordinary use, vessels and flasks from that kind out of bark.

The Blessed Virgin washed and dried some things here. Then, after having rested and refreshed themselves, they proceeded on their way by the common high road.

They made their journey without any special danger to them. Mary was often extremely distressed, because walking through the hot sand was so painful for the Boy Jesus. Joseph had made for Him, out of bark, shoes that reached above the ankle, where they were firmly fastened. Even so, the holy travelers frequently paused while Mary shook the sand out of the Child's shoes.

She herself wore sandals. Jesus was dressed in His little brown robe, and they often had to seat Him on the donkey. For protection against the scorching rays of the sun, all three wore broad hats made of bark and fastened under the chin with a string.

They passed by many cities and at last came to Gaza, where they stopped for three months. There were many pagans in that city. Joseph did not want to return to Nazareth, but to go to Bethlehem. Yet he was undecided, because Bethlehem was in Judea, and he had heard that Archelaus was now reigning over Judea—and that ruler was also quite cruel.

Then an angel appeared and put an end to his doubts by telling him that he should return to Nazareth. Anne was still living there. She and some of her relatives were the only ones that knew where the Holy Family had lived during those years.

The Boy Jesus walked between Mary and Joseph on their journey back to Judea from Egypt. The donkey was no longer with them then, so they had to carry their bundles themselves.

Once, as they walked on a road in the desert, they came to a place about two hours' distance from the cave of Jesus's young cousin, John. The young boy had been brought by his mother, Elizabeth, to live there to escape Herod's massacre. As Jesus walked, He gazed in that direction, and His soul was turning to John.

At the same time, John was at prayer in his cave. An angel in the form of a boy appeared to him, telling him that the Savior was passing by. John emerged from the cave and, with outstretched arms, ran in the direction of the place where his Savior was passing. He hopped about and danced with joy.

The Holy Family at last returned to their home in Nazareth. It had three separate rooms. The one belonging to the Mother of God was the largest and most pleasant; in it Jesus, Mary, and Joseph met to pray. They stood at prayer, with their hands crossed on their breast, and they spoke aloud.

They often prayed together under a lamp that had several wicks, or near a kind of branched candlestick fastened to the wall, where the flame burned. But most of the time they were alone in their respective rooms, with Joseph working in his. He was cutting sticks and lathes, planing wood, and carrying up a beam, with Jesus helping him.

Joseph ordered his occupations and his work in the way that would be most worthy to earn a livelihood to support the divine Child and His mother as well as for himself. What in other sons of Adam is considered a punishment and a hardship was to this holy patriarch a great happiness. For while others were condemned to sustain their natural life by the labor of their hands in the sweat of their brows, Joseph was blessed and consoled beyond measure to know that he had been chosen by his labor and sweat to support God Himself, to whom belonged heaven and earth and all that they contain, and God's own mother.

Mary was generally engaged sewing or knitting with little needles. She sat on the ground as she worked, with her feet crossed under her, and a little basket at her side.

The two slept alone, each in a separate room. Their beds consisted of blankets that were rolled up in the morning.

Sometimes, when Joseph worked very strenuously, he would approach his spouse and ask her to grant him the favor of singing for him a hymn in praise of God. That way her singing could relieve his fatigue. The holy Virgin would readily agree to fulfill his requests. Her singing of the hymns of divine exaltation was so delightful that Joseph was often carried into ecstasy.

He once remarked to Mary: "My spouse, your singing alone is enough to bring comfort to every afflicted heart! What consolation you gave me through it! What relief for my weariness! What a great joy it is for me to hear you speak or sing!"

These words gave the most holy Virgin an occasion for giving additional praise to God, the Source of all that is good. "God has poured these graces into my heart," she told him, "so that you might be comforted and obtain relief in your tribulations and afflictions." The saint's love and gratitude to God increased steadily, and he continued to wonder at the virtue of his most holy spouse.

As soon as Jesus grew up sufficiently to be capable of assisting Joseph in his carpentry, He would take the initiative to join His foster father at his work and to console him by His presence. We can well imagine what spiritual joy the happy Joseph must have known, and how deep his consolation, whenever he took the Child with him to work. When he labored with the Son of God Himself at his side, it seemed as if he were in paradise.

Sometimes, little Jesus would hand him tools; sometimes, pieces of lumber. He even worked hard to lift the heavier boards, because He wanted to work like a strong grownup. Joseph was deeply touched by His efforts and tried in every way he could to keep the Boy from overexerting Himself.

Jesus was most amiable, kind, and gracious, so other children tended to gather in the workshop just so they could enjoy His pleasant company. The Child gladly spent time with these youngsters, teaching them about the mysteries of the true Faith. Even adults came at times to the workshop with projects, just so they might have a chance to see Jesus and talk with Him.

This situation provided a considerable amount of work for Joseph, and he applied himself to their projects with great physical effort and determination. But little Jesus was there to help him, and His love for His foster father inspired and guided Him to anticipate his every little need. With His blessed little hands, He would wipe the sweat from Joseph's face, and He lightened the carpenter's burden of labor considerably.

Jesus assisted His parents in every possible way. He helped, as well, everyone He met on the street wherever an opportunity arose, cheerfully, eagerly, and obligingly. When He was not assisting His foster father in his trade, Jesus devoted Himself to prayer and contemplation. He was a model for all the children of Nazareth; they loved Him and feared displeasing Him.

When they were naughty and did wrong, their parents used to say to them: "What will Joseph's Son say when I tell Him this? How sorry He will be!"

Sometimes the parents gently complained to Jesus in the presence of the little ones, saying, "Tell them not to do such or such a thing anymore." Jesus took it playfully and like a little child. He would beg the children affectionately to do so and so, then He would pray with them to His Heavenly Father for strength to become better, persuading them to acknowledge their faults and ask pardon on the spot.

At the age of eight years, Jesus went for the first time with His parents to Jerusalem for the Passover, and every year afterward He did the same. In those first visits, Jesus had already attracted attention in Jerusalem among the friends with whom He and His parents stayed, and among the priests and doctors of the law as well. They spoke of the pious, intelligent Child, Joseph's extraordinary Son.

# CHAPTER THIRTEEN

# JESUS IN THE TEMPLE

BECAUSE of His previous annual pilgrimages, Jesus already had a few acquaintances in Jerusalem when, in His twelfth year, He accompanied His parents, with their friends and their sons, to the great city. His parents were accustomed to walk with the people from their own part of the country, and they knew that Jesus, who was now making the journey for the fifth time, always went with the other youths from Nazareth.

This time, however, Jesus had separated from His companions on the return journey not far from the Mount of Olives. They all thought that He had joined His parents who were following. But Jesus had gone to that side of Jerusalem nearest to Bethlehem, to the inn where the Holy Family had stayed before Mary's purification in the Temple. Mary and Joseph thought He had gone on ahead with the other Nazarenes.

When at last they all met at a small village on the way, Mary and Joseph discovered that Jesus was not among the other pilgrims, and their anxiety was intense. They returned at once to Jerusalem, making inquiries after Him on the way and everywhere in the city itself. But they could not find Him, since He had not been where they usually stayed. Jesus had instead slept at the inn before the Bethlehem gate, where the people knew Him and His parents.

There He had joined several youths and gone with them to two schools of the city, the first day to one, the second to another. On the morning of the third day, He had gone to a third school at the Temple, and in the afternoon into the Temple itself where His parents would eventually find Him. These schools were all different, and not all were strictly schools of the Law. Other studies were also taught in them.

The third school was in the neighborhood of the Temple, and from it, the Levites and priests were chosen. Jesus by His questions and answers astonished and embarrassed the doctors and rabbis of all these schools. So they resolved, on the afternoon of the third day, in the public lecture hall of the Temple and in the presence of the rabbis most deeply versed in the various studies, "to humble the Boy Jesus." The scribes and doctors had coordinated the plan together because, although pleased at first, they had in the end become annoyed at Him.

They met in the public lecture hall in the middle of the Temple porch in front of the Sanctuary, in the round place where years later Jesus Himself would teach. There our young Lord sat in a large chair that, because of his youth, He did not at all fill. Around Him was a crowd of aged Jews in priestly robes. They were listening attentively and appeared to be perfectly furious, eager to lay hands on Him.

On the top of the chair where Jesus was sitting were carved heads like those of dogs. They were greenish brown, the upper parts glistening and sparkling with a yellow light. There were similar heads and figures on several long tables that stood in the Temple sideways from this place, covered with offerings. The place was very large and so crowded that one could scarcely imagine himself in a sacred place.

In the schools, Jesus had illustrated His answers and explanations by all kinds of examples from nature, art, and science. So the scribes and doctors had diligently gathered together masters in all these branches of knowledge. They now began, one by one, to dispute with Him.

Jesus remarked that, properly speaking, such subjects did not appear appropriate to the Temple. Yet he agreed to discuss them since that was His Father's will. Even so, they did not understand that He referred to His Heavenly Father; they imagined that Joseph had commanded Him to show off His learning.

Jesus now answered and taught first about medicine. He described the whole human body in a way far beyond the reach of even the most learned. He spoke authoritatively with the same ease about astronomy, architecture, agriculture, geometry, arithmetic, jurisprudence, and, in short, about every subject proposed to Him.

He applied all these subjects so skillfully to the Law and the Promise, to the Prophecies, to the Temple, to the mysteries of worship and sacrifice, that His hearers were surprised and confounded. They passed from astonishment and admiration to fury and shame. The men were enraged at hearing some things that they had never known before, and at hearing others that they had never before understood.

Jesus had been teaching two hours when Joseph and Mary entered the Temple. They had inquired after their Child with the Levites whom they knew, who had answered that He was with the doctors in the lecture hall. But as they were not at liberty to enter that hall, they sent one of the Levites in to call Jesus.

Jesus sent them word that He must first finish what He was then doing. Mary was very much troubled at His not obeying at once, for this was the first time He had given His parents to understand that He had other commands than theirs to fulfill.

The Boy continued to teach for another hour. Then He left the hall and joined His parents in Solomon's Porch, on the eastern side of the Court of the Women, leaving His hearers confounded, confused, and enraged. Joseph was quite awed and astonished, but he kept a humble silence.

Mary, however, drawing near to Jesus, said, "Child, why have You done this to us? Your father and I have been looking for You anxiously!"

But Jesus answered gravely, "Why have you been looking for Me? Do you not know that I must be about My Father's business?" [Lk 2:48–49].

Still, they did not understand. They at once began with Him their journey home. The bystanders gazed at them in astonishment, looking as if they might lay hands upon the Boy, for some of them were full of rage. Even so, although the crowd was dense, a wide path was made to permit the Holy Family to pass in peace.

Jesus's teaching made a great impression upon the scribes. Some recorded the affair as a notable event, while here and there it was whispered around, giving rise to all kinds of remarks and false reports. But the true statement, the scribes kept to themselves. They spoke of Jesus as of a very brash boy, possessing fine talents indeed, but needing to have those talents cultivated.

The Holy Family again left the city. Outside of it, they joined a party of about three men, two women, and some children who were from Nazareth. They went together to different places around Jerusalem, and also to Mount Olivet. They wandered around the beautiful pleasure grounds found there, occasionally standing to pray, with their hands crossed on their breasts. They also crossed over a bridge that spanned a brook. The little party's walking around and praying was much like a pilgrimage.

When Jesus had returned to Nazareth, a feast was celebrated in Anne's house, where all the young men and women among their friends and relatives were gathered. It served as a feast of rejoicing that Jesus had been found, a feast solemnized on the return from the Paschal journey, and a feast customary on the completion of a son's twelfth year. Jesus was clearly the focus of the celebration.

Beautiful bowers were erected over the table, where garlands of vine leaves and sheaves of grain were hung. The children were served with grapes and little rolls. There were present at this feast thirty-three boys, all future disciples of Jesus.

During the whole feast, Jesus instructed the other boys and explained to them a very wonderful parable, but they understood it only imperfectly. It was of a marriage feast at which water could be turned into wine and the lukewarm guests into zealous friends; and again, of a marriage feast where the wine could be changed into Blood and the bread into Flesh, and that Blood and Flesh would remain with the guests until the end of the world as strength and consolation, as a living bond of union. He also said to one of the youths, a relative of His own named Nathanael: "I will be present at your marriage."

From His twelfth year, Jesus was always like a teacher among His companions. He often sat among them, instructing them or walking around the country with them.

As the Gospel says, Jesus was subject to His parents [Lk 2:57], and constantly in prayer. As He grew older, He worked with His hands. His features and His words were so wonderful and so pleasing that many people used to say when they had difficulties, "We should go to Mary's Son—He will console us!"

He talked with Mary and Joseph so inspiringly about God that they were continually filled with indescribable joy. And when they were in fear, in poverty, and in adversity, He did not miraculously produce gold and silver for them. Instead, He urged them to be patient, and they were marvelously preserved.

What the family needed was sometimes given to them by compassionate and devout souls. At other times, it came from their work. In this way, they had what they needed to live on, but nothing unnecessary, for they sought only to serve God.

At home, with friends who visited the family, Jesus talked confidently about the Law of God and its meanings and types. He openly debated with learned men, so that they were amazed and used to say, "Joseph's Son instructs the scribes—there is a great spirit in Him!"

Jesus was also so obedient that when Joseph said to Him, "Do this" or "Do that," He did it at once. For He concealed the power of His Divinity in such a way that it could only be perceived by Mary, and at times by Joseph. Very often they saw Him surrounded by a marvelous light and heard angels' voices singing over Him. They also observed that evil spirits, which could not be cast out by official exorcists, fled at the sight of His presence.

## CHAPTER FOURTEEN

# *JOSEPH'S LATER YEARS*

IN Joseph's later years, Jesus lived in total submission to His parents, seeking to conform to their desires in every way. But Joseph was terribly embarrassed to have his divine Son subject to him, especially now that He was almost a man. He humbled himself before God and acknowledged his own lowliness, asking that he himself might be made subject to Jesus instead. But God would not grant Joseph's wish in this matter, so the carpenter had to obey the divine will.

Throughout this time, Jesus never acted without Joseph's approval. He would not even leave the workshop to visit His mother without express permission from Joseph. The saint was astounded by the Savior's deep humility, and he sought to imitate His example. The sight of God Himself being submissive to Joseph's commands in this way pressed the carpenter to humble himself even more. Sometimes he would lovingly press his lips to those tools and other objects in the workshop that Jesus had touched with His sacred hands.

Meanwhile, Joseph's love and reverence for Mary continually increased, and he always desired to be with her. When he went to work, he regretted that he had to be separated from her, so that he could not see, hear, or talk with her. Jesus was with him, of course, but Joseph still yearned to be with Mary as well, because she was his dearest spouse, a creature of highest dignity and extraordinary virtue.

Even so, the carpenter never allowed her to see his feelings in this regard. When he left her to go to work, he would go with full resignation. And he would often overcome his impulses to stop working and visit her, offering this sacrifice to the Lord.

Yet Jesus knew that the loving Joseph had this holy yearning. So He often found ways to send Joseph to Mary, providing consolation for his spirit. He wanted His foster father to have such a consolation in addition to the one that He Himself provided by His own presence.

Whenever Joseph saw Mary, his love of God grew stronger, and his heart would come alive with a hunger for greater holiness. For the Mother of God possessed this special privilege: When someone gazed upon her with a true and chaste love (as Joseph certainly did), that person would be filled through and through with a holy zeal and heavenly longings.

At the same time, Joseph was acutely aware of the great pleasure Mary took in seeing her Jesus. So he sometimes would look for opportunities to ask Jesus to leave His work and go to her. Whenever he had a message for his spouse, for example, he would send Jesus to relay it to His holy mother, instructing Him to stay with her as long as He wished. The youth would then obediently seek out His mother and grant her the consolation of His presence and His divine words, conversing with her in a mutual exchange of affection.

Such consolations in Joseph's life were accompanied by tribulations as well. Some who visited the workshop to catch a glimpse of Jesus made comments that were well intentioned but disparaged the saint. They could not comprehend, they said, how Joseph had the heart to insist that such a Son—dignified, gracious, and handsome—must spend His time working so hard in the shop.

A young Man with such a remarkable disposition and extraordinary talents should be allowed to study the Scriptures, they said. Then He would grow up to become an eminent doctor of the Law. Certainly, He would be a success and bring honor to His people.

These comments pierced Joseph's heart. He said nothing, but looked downward while they accused him of lacking love for his Son and consideration for the weakness of His youth. On fire with zeal, they scolded him for being, as they thought, thoughtless, cruel, and hard of heart, indifferent to the Youth's burden in working such a trade. They insisted that if anyone else had a son so remarkable and gifted, such a father would even risk his life in laboring to increase his earnings so that his Son could have the means to engage in these studies.

Joseph heard these words with sincere anguish, humbling himself. He knew that as merely human judgments, their accusations were correct. But he could not shed the necessary light on the situation for them to understand, because God had not granted him permission to reveal His secret about Jesus's identity.

With deep humility and deference, Joseph conceded that they were correct. But he added that, considering how much he needed the help of the Son that God had given him, he could not very well deprive himself of it. If he should ever find out that the Lord actually desired otherwise, he would be eager to do God's will.

Then they mocked him, saying: "So you want us to believe that God Himself tells you what to do? How presumptuous! No matter what, you should just let your Son study!"

The saint bowed his head and said no more. He suffered their persistent demands with unyielding patience and gave them no reason to take offense. Even though they deserved a rebuke for their rudeness, he thanked them for their attention to his situation and their interest in his Son.

But his patience only provoked their conclusion that he was obstinate and refused to be persuaded. So they spread their accusations against Joseph throughout the village, and continued to harass him this way every time they entered his shop. Nevertheless, Joseph took this as another opportunity to practice virtue, and he prayed for his tormenters.

At the same time, the carpenter's heart was especially sensitive to these accusations because he felt grieved that Jesus had to engage in such drudgery in his poor workshop. He wept many tears in his anguish, but he steadfastly conformed his desires to God's will.

With smiling glances, young Jesus let his adoptive father know His pleasure in seeing such virtue in him. These were all that Joseph needed to be consoled. Looking at his beautiful Son, he felt a joy without compare rise up in his heart, and he would say: "My dear Son, just a glance from You is enough to make every bitterness sweet for me! Just a glimpse of You, my beloved Jesus, is enough to lift up my soul! Even if I should be afflicted by trials, even if I should be despised and mocked, humiliated and persecuted, all these things will grow delightful and pleasurable for me if I look at You, my most precious Good!"

The saint's devotion to the mystery of the Incarnation remained deep and fervent throughout the last years of his life. Ever since he had found out from Mary the day and hour that this miracle was announced to her by the angel, he commemorated the event with celebrations every month and year. Joseph would prepare himself for these occasions by taking on strict disciplines. When the anniversary arrived, he would rise and pray at the hour when this great mystery took place, thanking God, along with Mary, on behalf of all the human race for the great Gift that was given to the world.

In a similar way, Joseph honored the mystery of Jesus's nativity. On the anniversary of that event, he rose at midnight because that was the time when the wondrous birth had taken place. Then he spent the remainder of the night meditating on this mystery and thanking God for it.

Joseph also cherished a devotion that commemorated Jesus's presentation in the Temple. He would contemplate the words spoken at that time by the aged and holy prophet Simeon.

Through these devotions, Joseph acquired considerable merit. He carried them out with great fervor and with such an abundance of tears shed that his heart seemed indeed to be melting away. Mary joined him in these devotions.

As the two of them engaged in holy conversation, their hearts grew more and more aflame with love for God. In these times, they often studied passages in the Holy Scriptures that indicated that the Savior would suffer tribulations. Mary explained these more fully to Joseph, and he understood perfectly all that she said. Joseph loved Jesus so much that his pains and bitter anguish grew even more intense when he considered again the afflictions that his beloved Savior would one day endure.

The love of God achieved such an intensity within Joseph that his body felt its affects. His heart became like a volcano of fiery, divine love, and he would often exclaim: "God of love! Make an end of my life! If only this fire of love aflame in my breast would consume me totally!" In fact, the saint became controlled by a fervent yearning for death because he was so fiercely aflame and consumed with divine love.

Joseph often looked at Jesus and meditated on His wondrous beauty; at times he was totally enraptured by it. Sometimes the thought of Jesus's afflictions to come would suddenly come to mind so that he whispered to himself: "Most beautiful, most extraordinary, most loving face of my Jesus! What anguish and sorrow will You express when You are outraged by Your creatures!"

Joseph's thoughts ran along the same lines whenever he meditated on the hands, the feet, or the breast of Jesus. Whenever the Savior spoke to him, revealing His supreme wisdom and concern, Joseph would whisper: "O divine mouth! The words of life come forth from You! Jesus, what a bitter cup You will have to drink. And how many who hear You will contradict Your divine words and heavenly teaching!"

Thoughts such as these were like swords piercing and severing Joseph's heart in two. He was gradually consumed by his love and suffering. As Jesus grew older, thoughts about His sufferings pressed themselves increasingly on Joseph's mind. Now, as the time of the Savior's bitter passion drew closer, his anguish intensified.

The carpenter's increasing agony over the future sufferings of the Savior, along with his increasing love for God, reached such a degree that his physical strength became seriously diminished, and his work became a severe burden. He seemed to be exhausted and depressed, so Jesus was conscientious in coming to his assistance. The young Man took on Himself the most difficult labors, making Joseph's work lighter.

Our Lord's mere presence was enough to console and strengthen His adoptive father. It enabled him to accomplish at least the lighter work. Jesus's sincere, compassionate words refreshed Joseph and kindled within him an even deeper love for the young Man.

Once, when Jesus grew weary from the difficult work, Joseph told Him: "My beloved Son! Today You labor to craft this wood. But the day is coming when other men will labor to prepare a cross of wood on which You will die."

With these words Joseph almost passed out, but Jesus quickly steadied and supported him in His arms. The young Man consoled him and reminded him that he must be conformed to God's will in all things. When Joseph heard these words, he sighed deeply and cried out: "Yes, yes, my Jesus! Let everything truly be accomplished according to God's will. Even so, my heart cannot escape such deep anguish, so I offer up to the Heavenly Father all my sorrow, together with my whole being. I would willingly die on a cross if that were His will."

Joseph was discouraged by the increasing loss of his physical strength. He was grieved that he could no longer perform the necessary labor to provide for his family's needs. One day, he said to Jesus with great tenderness: "My precious Son and Lord! How it hurts to see you toil so tirelessly, while I can only stand by, offering so little help. My only desire now is to be strong enough to assist you even in small ways so I can offer you at least a little relief. Even so, I feel so weak. It seems that I am unworthy to be allowed to work, as I used to do, on Your behalf."

But Jesus began to comfort him, recalling that the carpenter had actually labored tirelessly in the past, doing all he could. So he should now be at peace, since it was only right for him to rest a little sometimes. Jesus encouraged him to bear his condition with good cheer, since his weak condition was God's will.

Consoled in this way, Joseph resigned himself graciously to his loss of physical capacity. His spiritual capacity, however, grew all the stronger. He was able to practice all the virtues with perfection and make great strides forward in grace and in love for his God.

Now that the carpenter found himself more and more incapable of physical labor, he began to contemplate deeply the perfect attributes of God. He was enflamed with a fervent desire for death so that he could have the perfect blessedness of seeing God face to face. His eyes would look again and again upward toward heaven and remain there for hours at a time.

Joseph longed for the day when the redemption of our race would be accomplished, knowing that through this redemption, he himself would become fit to enter the Father's mansions in heaven. He recited passages of Scripture and the Psalms of David that expressed this holy longing.

Despite his condition, the saint maintained his daily custom of prayers. In fact, he multiplied his prayers, spending many hours on his knees. He often begged the Father to grant that all would accept the coming Messiah when He was revealed. And he frequently said to himself, "How blessed will be those who hear the word of God and keep it!" [Lk 11:28].

Joseph said to Mary: "My dear spouse, it will be your high privilege to hear our Jesus preach. But you will have a great burden of bitterness to bear as you watch the horrible suffering, opposition, and persecution He will have to endure. His divine words will give you comfort, and His loving care will give you strength."

Despite Joseph's feeble condition, he continued to go with Jesus each day to the workshop. "My beloved Savior," he told Him, "let me be with you, because I know I have only a little while left on this earth. I want to enjoy Your dear presence as long as I can, because I will no longer have the privilege of seeing You after I die, until You enter Limbo triumphantly to set free my soul and the souls of the Patriarchs and the other righteous people of old." Jesus agreed to let Joseph be with him, knowing what joy it brought him.

Joseph often asked Jesus to tell him about heavenly things and the mysteries of His life, passion, and death. Our Lord was happy to grant his request by talking about the mysteries of His incarnation, the perfect attributes of God, and the glories of heaven. All this increased the saint's desire to depart from this life to enjoy the full and unobscured vision of God.

# CHAPTER FIFTEEN

# *THE DEATH OF JOSEPH*

A S the time drew nearer for Jesus to begin His mission of teaching, Joseph continued to decline. God led him along the path of suffering, in imitation of the way of the Cross. The Lord loved Joseph above all the sons of men. In order to increase his merits and crown before the time of his meriting should come to an end, He visited him in the last years of his life with certain sicknesses, such as fever, violent headaches, and very painful arthritis, which greatly afflicted and weakened him.

In the midst of these infirmities, as we have seen, Joseph was suffering from another source. It was sweeter, but extremely painful: The fire of his ardent love was so vehement, the flights and ecstasies of his most pure soul would often have burst the bounds of his body if the Lord, who granted them, had not strengthened and comforted him against these agonies of love. In these sweet overflows, the Lord allowed him to suffer until his death. On account of the natural weakness of his emaciated body, this experience was the source of indescribable merits for the fortunate saint, not only because of the sufferings endured, but because of the love by which these sufferings were brought about.

One day God chose to test the saint's faithfulness by allowing Satan to test him. He was subjected to an assault of excruciating pain and gravely tempted to impatience and despair. Even so, Joseph persisted in his faithfulness to God and displayed an invincible patience. He conquered the enemy through his unflinching courage and by stirring himself up to acts of faith in God, even when it appeared that God had abandoned him. He persevered in appealing to God's mercy and generosity, with an abiding conviction that the Lord would come to his assistance. In this way, Joseph practiced heroic virtue in this spiritual battle.

After the saint had endured this great trial for several hours, he entrusted himself earnestly to God. Then Jesus came to visit him, and when He did, the Devil fled at the sight, confused and vanquished by the virtue that Joseph had practiced. With Our Lord's help, he was delivered from further temptations, and his pain was somewhat relieved.

Joseph then grew calm and was able to sleep a little. Later, when Mary had come to him, he told her everything he had been suffering. She continued to urge him to bear his condition with cheerfulness and courage, because God's purpose in this trial was to flood him with merits and make him exceptionally great in His kingdom.

Our great Queen was a witness to all that was happening within Joseph's soul. She rejoiced in her knowledge of having for her spouse a man so holy and so beloved of the Lord. She beheld and comprehended the sincerity and purity of his soul; his burning love; his exalted and heavenly thoughts; his dove-like patience and meekness in his grievous ailments and intense sufferings.

Mary reassured her spouse that God had given the saint His grace and had not at all abandoned him. In truth, the Lord had always remained beside him, granting him the strength to endure his trials. And God, she insisted, was extremely pleased by his steadfastness and faithfulness.

She knew that Joseph never complained either of these trials nor of any others, nor did he ever ask for any relief in his poverty and necessities. He bore it all with incomparable composure and greatness of soul. As his spouse contemplated and weighed all these heroic virtues of Joseph, she came to look upon him with a reverence that no one can imagine.

Meanwhile, Mary labored with remarkable joy for Joseph's support and comfort, and the greatest of his comforts was that she could prepare and serve him his food with her own pure hands. But as all her service seemed too little in the eyes of the heavenly Lady compared to the needs of her spouse, she sometimes, in her love for him, made use of her power as the Queen and mistress of all creation: She would command the food she gave him to impart special strength and supply new life to the holy and just man of God.

When this command of the great Lady, whom all creatures obeyed, was fulfilled, Joseph tasted the food that bore these blessings of sweetness. He perceived their effects and was moved to say to the Queen: "My Lady and spouse, what heavenly food is this that gives me life, brings joy to my senses, restores my strength, and fills my soul and spirit with new delight?"

Though she was the Empress of heaven, she kneeled to serve Joseph his meals; and when he was disabled and suffering, she knelt as well to take off his shoes. At other times she held him in her arms. Although the humble Joseph sought to rouse himself to prevent some of these acts of service she performed, he could not altogether prevent them, for she was intimately aware of all his sufferings and weaknesses, and of the circumstances and occasions when he needed her help.

Often as well, as the mistress of wisdom and virtue, she comforted him by words of sweetest consolation. At the end of his life, when his infirmities increased, our Queen assisted him day and night, and her only other concern was the service and ministry she owed to her most holy Son. Jesus sometimes joined and assisted her in the care of Joseph whenever He was not engaged in other necessary work for their livelihood.

There was never a person, nor will there ever be one, who was so well nursed and comforted as was Joseph. The happiness of this man of God was great, for he alone deserved to have for his spouse the one who was the spouse of the Holy Spirit.

Even so, the heavenly lady was not satisfied with these proofs of her devotion toward Joseph. Mary made use of other means for his relief and comfort. Several times she asked the Lord in her fervent love to impose on her the pains suffered by her spouse, releasing him from them. She pled the sanctity of Joseph, his purity, innocence, and delight in the Lord in this heart made like the heart of her Son. She asked for many blessings for him and gave most heartfelt thanks to God for having created a man so worthy of His favors, so full of justice and holiness.

Our Lady invited the holy angels to give thanks to God for Joseph, and in contemplating the glory and wisdom of the Lord as displayed in this man, she sang new hymns of praise. For on one hand she saw the pains and sufferings of her beloved spouse, which stirred her pity and compassion. On the other hand, she was aware of his merits and the delight of the Lord in this man, and how the saint pleased and glorified his God by his patience.

Sometimes, when the merciful Queen perceived the bitterness and severity of the sufferings of Joseph, she was moved to tender pity. Then she would humbly ask permission of her most holy Son to be allowed to command the natural sources and occasions of these pains to disappear, thus putting a stop to the sufferings of this just and beloved man of God. Since all creatures obeyed the command of their great mistress, her holy spouse was then immediately relieved and rested from his pains, sometimes for a day, sometimes longer, until his ailments, according to the decree of the Almighty, again took hold to bring about the increase of his merits.

At other times Mary instructed the holy angels, as their Queen (though not in the form of a command, but of a request), to console Joseph and comfort him in his sorrows and labors, as the frail condition of his body demanded. At that request, the angelic spirits would appear to Joseph in human forms, most beautiful and shining. They would begin to speak to him about God and His infinite perfections.

Then they would raise their voices in the sweetest harmony of celestial music, singing hymns of divine canticles, through which they restored Joseph's drooping strength and inflamed the love of his purest soul. To move his spirit to rejoice even more, he was informed in particular not only of the source of these particular blessings and divine favors, but of the great holiness of his virginal spouse, of her unequaled love and charity in conversing with him and serving him, and of many other excellences and privileges of the great mistress of the world. All this together caused such effects in Joseph, and so raised his merits before God, that no tongue can express them, nor can any human understanding in this life comprehend them.

Joseph was subject to infirmities and sufferings for several years, and his noble soul was purified more and more each day in the crucible of affliction and of divine love. As the time passed, his bodily strength gradually diminished, and he approached the unavoidable end, in which the debt of death is paid by all of us children of Adam [Heb 9:27]. In a similar way, the care and solicitude of his heavenly spouse, our queen, increased as she assisted and served him with prompt and constant care in every detail.

Perceiving, in her exalted wisdom, that the day and hour for his departure from this cumbersome earth was very near, the loving Lady went to her blessed Son and said to Him: "Lord God Most High, Son of the eternal Father and Savior of the world, by Your divine light I see the hour approaching which You have decreed for the death of Your servant Joseph. I beg You, by Your ancient mercies and by Your infinite bounty, to assist him in that hour by Your almighty power. Let his death be as precious in Your eyes as the uprightness of his life was pleasing to You so that he may depart in peace and in the certain hope of the eternal reward to be given to him on the day in which You will open the gates of heaven for all the faithful.

"Be mindful, my Son, of the humility and love of Your servant, of his surpassingly great merits and virtues, and of the faithfulness and consideration by which this just man has supported You and me, Your humble handmaid, by the sweat of his brow."

Our Savior answered: "My mother, your request is pleasing to Me, and the merits of Joseph are acceptable in My eyes. I will now assist him and will assign him a place among the princes of My people, so high that he will be the admiration of the angels and will cause them and all people to break forth in highest praise. With none other will I do as with your spouse."

The great Lady gave thanks to her sweetest Son for this promise. Then, for nine days and nights before the death of Joseph he uninterruptedly enjoyed the company and assistance of either Mary or her divine Son. By command of the Lord the holy angels, three times on each of the nine days, furnished celestial music, mixing their hymns of praise with the benedictions of the sick man. In addition, their humble but most precious home was filled with the sweetest fragrance and aromas so wonderful that they not only comforted Joseph but also invigorated all the many people who happened to come near the house.

One day before he died, being wholly inflamed with divine love on account of these blessings, Joseph was wrapped in an ecstasy that lasted twenty-four hours. The Lord Himself supplied strength for this miraculous interchange. In this ecstasy he saw clearly the divine Essence and, manifested in that vision, all that he had believed by faith: the incomprehensible Divinity, the mystery of the Incarnation and Redemption, the militant Church with all its sacraments and mysteries. At that time, the Blessed Trinity commissioned and assigned him as the messenger of our Savior to the holy patriarchs and prophets in Limbo, commanding him to prepare them for their coming forth from this bosom of Abraham to eternal rest and happiness.

All this most holy Mary saw reflected in the Soul of her divine Son together with all the other mysteries, just as they had been made known to her beloved spouse. For all this she offered her sincerest thanks to her Lord.

When Joseph emerged from this ecstasy, his face shone with wonderful splendor, and his soul was entirely transformed by his vision of the essence of God. He asked his blessed spouse to give him her benediction. But she asked her divine Son to bless him in her stead, which He did.

Then the great Queen of humility, falling on her knees, asked Joseph to bless her, since he was her husband and head. Under divine impulse, the man of God fulfilled this request for the consolation of his most prudent spouse. She kissed the hand with which he blessed her and asked him to greet the righteous ones of Limbo in her name.

The most humble Joseph, sealing his life with an act of self-abasement, asked pardon of his heavenly spouse for all his deficiencies in her service and love, and he begged her to grant him her assistance and intercession in this hour of his passing away. The holy man also rendered humblest thanks to her Son for all the blessings of his life and especially for those received during this sickness. The last words that Joseph spoke to his spouse were these: "Blessed are you among all women, and chosen of all creatures. Let angels and men praise you; let all the generations know, praise, and exalt your dignity; and may the name of the Most High be known, adored, and exalted in you through all the coming ages. May He be eternally praised for having created you so pleasing in His eyes and in the sight of all the blessed spirits. I hope to enjoy the sight of you in the heavenly fatherland."

Then this man of God, turning toward Christ, Our Lord, in the most profound reverence, wished to kneel before Him. But the sweetest Jesus, coming near, took him in His arms, where Joseph lay down his head, saying: "My highest Lord and God, Son of the eternal Father, Creator and Redeemer of the World, give Your blessing to Your servant and the works of Your hands. Pardon, O most merciful King, the faults that I have committed in Your service and dealings with me. I extol and magnify You. I render eternal and heartfelt thanks to You for having, in Your condescension beyond words, chosen me to be the spouse of Your true mother. Let Your greatness and glory be my thanksgiving for all eternity."

The Redeemer of the world then gave him His benediction, saying: "My father, rest in peace and in the grace of my eternal Father and my grace. To the prophets and saints, who await you in Limbo, bring the joyful news of the approach of their redemption."

At these words of Jesus, and lying in His arms, the most fortunate Joseph breathed his last, and the Lord Himself closed his eyes. At the same time, the multitude of the angels who attended upon their King and queen intoned hymns of praise in loud and harmonious voices. By command of the Lord they carried his most holy soul to the gathering place of the patriarchs and prophets.

There he was immediately recognized by all as clothed in the splendors of incomparable grace. As the presumed father and the intimate friend of the Redeemer, they knew Him to be worthy of highest veneration. In accordance with the will and mandate of the Lord, his arrival spread unutterable joy in this countless gathering of the saints by the announcement of their fast-approaching rescue.

After his death, his hands were crossed on his breast, and he was wrapped from head to foot in a white winding sheet, laid in a narrow casket, and placed in a very beautiful tomb, the gift of a good man. Only a few men followed the coffin with Jesus and Mary, but it was accompanied by angels and surrounded by light. Joseph's remains were afterward removed by the Christians to Bethlehem and interred there, still lying there today incorrupt.

Mary of course felt the natural sorrow due to the death of Joseph. She loved him as her spouse, as a man preeminent in perfection and holiness, and as her protector and benefactor.

# CHAPTER SIXTEEN

# THE SPECIAL VIRTUES, GRACES, AND GLORIES OF JOSEPH

IN God's providence, Joseph had to die before Jesus did, because Joseph could not have endured His crucifixion; he was too gentle, too loving. He had already suffered much from the persecution Jesus had had to endure from the malice of the people from His twentieth to His thirtieth year; for they could not bear the sight of Him. Their jealousy often made them exclaim that the carpenter's Son thought He knew everything better than others, that He was frequently at variance with the teachings of the Pharisees, and that He always had around Him a crowd of young followers.

In addition, the Lord had given him great knowledge of the Holy Scriptures and of prophecy so that he knew all that the Redeemer would have to suffer. The cross that Jesus had ever before Him in His thoughts from the first moment of His conception, Joseph too had present in his mind, and his soul was pierced by it. For this reason, while holding the Most Holy Lord in his arms, and often reflecting on all He would have to endure, Joseph's tears poured down. At other times, while keeping the Babe folded in his arms when it was cold, Joseph would warm His sacred hands by breathing on them.

We must note, then, that the long sickness and sufferings that preceded the death of Joseph were not the sole cause and occasion of his passing away. For with all his infirmities, he could have extended the term of his life if to these infirmities he had not joined the fire of the intense love within his breast. So that his death might be more the triumph of his love than the effects of original sin, the Lord suspended the special and miraculous assistance by which Joseph's natural forces had been enabled to withstand the violence of his love during his lifetime.

As soon as this divine assistance was withdrawn, his nature was overcome by his love. The bonds and chains by which this most holy soul was detained in its mortal body were at once dissolved, and the separation of the soul from the body that is death took place. Love was then the real cause of the death of Joseph. This was at the same time the greatest and most glorious of all his infirmities; for him, death was but a sleep of the body and the beginning of real life.

There is a certain difference in the graces given to this great patriarch and those granted to other saints. For many saints were endowed with graces and gifts that are intended not for the increase of their own sanctity but for the advance of the service of the Most High in other souls. They were, so to say, gifts and graces freely given and not dependent upon the holiness of the receiver.

But in our blessed patriarch, all the divine favors were productive of personal virtue and perfection; for the mysterious purpose, toward which they tended and helped along, was closely connected with the holiness of his own life. The more angelic and holy he grew to be, the more worthy he was to be the spouse of most holy Mary, the depository and treasury of heavenly mysteries. He was to be a miracle of holiness, as he really was.

For the confirmation and increase of Joseph's good qualities was then added the intercession of the blessed Lady. For as soon as she was informed that the Lord wished her to enter the married state with him, she earnestly sought the Lord to sanctify him and inspire him with most chaste thoughts and desires in accordance with her own. The Lord listened to her prayer and permitted her to see what great effects His right hand worked in the mind and spirit of the patriarch Joseph.

These effects were so abundant that they cannot be described in human words. God infused into his soul the most perfect habits of all the virtues and gifts. He balanced anew all his faculties and filled him with grace, confirming it in an admirable manner.

In the virtue and perfection of chastity this holy spouse was elevated higher than the seraphim; for the purity that they possessed without a body, Joseph possessed in his earthly body and in mortal flesh. Never did an image of the impurities of the lower nature of the senses engage, even for one moment, any of his faculties. This freedom from all such imaginations, and his angelic simplicity, fitted him for the companionship and presence of the purest among all creatures, and without this excellence he would not have been worthy of so great a dignity and rare excellence.

So perfectly was he dead to the world and the flesh, he desired nothing but the things of heaven. In the other virtues as well he was wonderfully distinguished, especially in charity. For he dwelled at the fountainhead of the living water that flows on to eternal life [Jn 4:14]. He was in close proximity to that sphere of fire and was consumed without resistance.

The manner of Joseph's death was a privilege of his unique love, for his sweet sighs of love surpassed and finally put an end to those of his sickness, being far more powerful. Because the objects of his love, Christ and His Mother, were present with him always, and both of them were more closely bound to him than to any others of those born to women, his most pure and faithful heart was inevitably consumed by the loving effects of such a close union.

Blessed be the Author of such great wonders, and blessed be the most fortunate of mortals, Joseph, who so worthily corresponded to their love! He deserves to be known and extolled by all generations of all nations, since the Lord has worked such things with no other man, and to none has He shown such love.

All the perfections distributed among so many princes were united in Joseph. The generous hand of the Creator poured forth in abundance upon this great saint all the qualities of body and soul. In this way he was made worthy to become the spouse of the Queen of angels and of the human race; the presumed father of the little Messiah; and the teacher of the divine Apprentice, who during so many years deigned to work under his direction in the humble workshop in Nazareth.

The divine visions and revelations granted to Joseph were many more than can be described, and the greatest of them all was his having known the mysteries of the relationship between Christ and His Mother, and his having lived in their company for so many years as the presumed father of the Lord and as the true spouse of the Queen of heaven. But there are yet more privileges conferred on Joseph by the Most High on account of his great holiness, which are especially important to those who ask his intercession in a proper manner.

In virtue of these special privileges, the intercession of Joseph is most powerful: first, for attaining the virtue of purity and overcoming the sensual inclinations of the flesh; second, for procuring powerful help to escape sin and return to the friendship of God; third, for increasing love and devotion to most holy Mary; fourth, for securing the grace of a happy death and protection against the demons in that hour; fifth, for inspiring the demons with terror at the mere mention of his name by those who seek his assistance; sixth, for gaining health of body and assistance in all kinds of difficulties; seventh, for obtaining children in families. These and many other favors God grants to those who properly and with good disposition seek the intercession of Joseph, the spouse of our Queen.

Let all the faithful children of the Church be deeply devoted to him. For they will experience these favors in reality if they dispose themselves as they should in order to receive and be fit for them.

# SOURCES

*The various threads woven together to form this narrative were adapted from the following sources:*

Baij, Maria Caecilia. *Das Leben des heiligen Josef.* German edition, translated by Ferdinand Kröpfl. Reprint, Stein am Rhein, Switzerland: Christiana Verlag, 2003.

———. *The Life of Saint Joseph.* Translated by Hubert J. Mark. Asbury, NJ: The 101 Foundation, 1997.

———. *Vita di san Giuseppe,* 2nd ed. Montefiascone, Italy.: Monastero di San Pietro, 1974.

Bridget of Sweden. *Revelations of St. Bridget on the Life and Passion of Our Lord and the Life of His Blessed Mother.* Fresno, CA: Apostolate of Christian Action, 1965. Reprint, Rockford, IL: TAN Books, 1984.

Brown, Raphael, comp. *The Life of Mary as Seen by the Mystics.* 1951. Reprint, Charlotte, NC: TAN Books, 1991.

Calloway, Donald H. *Consecration to St. Joseph: The Wonders of Our Spiritual Father.* Stockbridge, MA: Marian Press, 2020.

Chorpenning, Joseph F. *Just Man, Husband of Mary, Guardian of Christ: An Anthology of Readings from Jeronimo Gracian's Summary of the Excellencies of St. Joseph,* 2^nd ed. Philadelphia: Saint Joseph's University Press, 1993.

de Ágreda, María de Jesús. *Mística ciudad de Dios: milagro de su omnipotencia y abismo de la gracia* ... Barcelona: Libería Religiosa, 1860.

de Ponte, Luis. *Vida Maravillosa de la Venerable Virgen Marina de Escobar.* Madrid: Joachin Ibarra, 1766.

Emmerich, Anne Catherine. *The Life of Jesus Christ and Biblical Revelations from the Visions of Blessed Anne Catherine Emmerich as recorded in the journals of Clemens Brentano.* Edited by Carl E. Schmöger, translated by Michael Palairet. 1914. Reprint, Charlotte, NC: TAN Books, 2011.

———. *The Life of the Blessed Virgin Mary from the Visions of Blessed Anne Catherine Emmerich.* Translated by Michael Palairet. 1914. Reprint, Rockford, IL: TAN Books, 1970.

*Favorite Prayers to St. Joseph.* Charlotte, NC: TAN Books, 2009.

*The History of Joseph the Carpenter,* in *The Ante-Nicene Fathers: Translations of the Fathers Down to A.D. 325,* vol. 3, *Fathers of the Third and Fourth Centuries.* 1886. Reprint, Grand Rapids, MI: William B. Eerdmans, 1986.

Mares, Courtney. "How a Forgotten Nun's Visions Shed 'New Light' on the Life of St. Joseph." *Catholic News Service,* March 16, 2021. https://angelusnews.com/faith/how-a-forgotten -nuns-visions-shed-new-light-on-the-life-of-st-joseph/.

Mary of Ágreda. *The Mystical City of God: Popular Abridgement of the Divine History and Life of the Virgin Mother of God.* Compiled by Cassian Burgert, translated by George J. Blatter. 1978. Reprint, Charlotte, NC: TAN Books, 2013.

———. *The Mystical City of God: The Divine History and Life of the Virgin Mother of God.* Translated by George J. Blatter. 1912. Reprint, Charlotte, NC: TAN Books, 2013.

Patrignani, Father. *A Manual of Practical Devotion to St. Joseph.* 1865. Reprint, Charlotte, NC: TAN Books, 1982.

Thompson, Edward Healy. *The Life and Glories of Saint Joseph: Husband of Mary, Foster-Father of Jesus, and Patron of the Universal Church.* 1888. Reprint, Charlotte, NC: TAN Books, 2013.

Turton, Rosalie A., ed. *St. Joseph as Seen by Mystics and Historians.* Asbury, NJ: The 101 Foundation, 2000.

# OTHER RECOMMENDED READING

Aquilina, Mike. *St. Joseph and His World.* New York: Scepter, 2000.

Binet, Père. *The Divine Favors Granted to St. Joseph.* 1973. Reprint, Rockford, IL: TAN Books, 1983.

Caster, Gary. *The Man Who Raised Jesus.* Cincinnati, OH: Servant Books, 2013.

Hicks, Boniface. *Through the Heart of St. Joseph.* Steubenville, OH: Emmaus Road, 2021.

John Paul II, Pope. Apostolic Exhortation *Redemptoris Custos (Guardian of the Redeemer).* Vatican City: Libreria Editrice Vaticana, 1989. https://www.vatican.va/content/john-paul-ii/en/apost_exhortations/documents/hf_jp-ii_exh_15081989_redemptoris-custos.html.

Le Tourneau, Dominique. *To Know St. Joseph: What Catholic Tradition Teaches About the Man Who Raised God.* El Cajon, CA: Catholic Answers Press, 2021.

Meschler, Maurice. *The Truth About St. Joseph: Encountering the Most Hidden of Saints.* Manchester, NH: Sophia Press, 2013.

Philippe, Marie-Dominique. *The Mystery of Joseph.* Bethesda, MD: Zaccheus Press, 2009.

Russell, Matthew. *Saint Joseph of Jesus and Mary.* 1898. Reprint, Affinity Imprints, 2021.